A Wee Nip at the 19th Hole

A History of the St. Andrews Caddie

by
RICHARD MACKENZIE

Sleeping Bear Press
Chelsea, Michigan

First published in the United States of America

October 1997
by
Sleeping Bear Press
121 South Main Street
PO Box 20
Chelsea, MI 48118

Text Copyright © Richard Mackenzie 1997
Photographs Copyright © The Royal & Ancient Golf Club, St. Andrews
University Library, St. Andrews Preservation Trust, Peter Adamson, Heiner
Kupcke, Iain Macfarlane Lowe, The Evening Telegraph-Dundee, and
Richard Mackenzie

First Impression October 1997

Library of Congress CIP Data on File

ISBN 1-886947-38-4

Cover photo: A group of caddies standing outside the R&A, circa 1890. Dan
Ferguson, caddie and golf professional, is on the far left. Professionals like Dan
were now being recognised by the Club with increased caddie tariffs and the
added bonus of tuition fees to supplement their income. The professional was
now becoming distinct from the ordinary caddie.

Typeset in Great Britain by Kirklane Ltd.
Edinburgh and St. Andrews

Printed in the United States of America

ACKNOWLEDGEMENTS

I am grateful to the many people who have given freely of their time to help make this book happen.

Michael Bonallack, Secretary of the Royal & Ancient Golf Club, and Lachlan McIntosh, Administration Secretary for the R&A, both facilitated my acquisition of Club records, photographs and documents, and encouraged me in my endeavour. The Royal & Ancient Golf Club kindly gave me permission to use these valuable materials in the book.

Peter Lewis, Director of the British Golf Museum, also gave me access to materials and invaluable encouragement. Fiona Grieve, Curator, and Elinor Clark, Assistant Curator, helped greatly by patiently searching for materials, and Hilary Webster, Visitor Services Manager, provided both tea and good cheer.

The St. Andrews Links Trust, with their continued development of the Caddie Department, have provided a good basis for my interaction with so many members of the international golfing community, and this has also become part of the formative planning of the book.

Jim Moore and especially John Di Falco and Bob McCrum offered their friendship and early support, and Bob in particular was an unfailing motivator. And more than anything, I want to thank all of the St. Andrews caddies, both past and present, who inspired me to give them their place in the history of this royal and ancient game.

Finally, I wish to thank my editor Marcia Julius, without whose skill and hard work this book would not have taken the form it has.

FOREWORD

Anyone who plays the Old Course for the first time without having a St. Andrews Caddie is as unprepared as one who sets out to climb Mount Everest without a guide.

Not only will the round be made easier, and safer on the nerves, but also it will be an enjoyable and educational experience.

For over two hundred years, caddies have been walking the most famous piece of golfing land in the world, advising players of vastly different abilities, not only on the club to take, but also on the type of shot required and, most importantly on the Old Course, exactly the line on which to play.

In this highly readable and enjoyable book, Rick Mackenzie reminds us how caddies first came to St. Andrews, the way in which they have added so much to the folklore of the links and the great contribution which they have made and continue to make to the game of golf for the benefit of those who visit "The Home of Golf".

Long may they continue their work for generations to come.

M. F. BONALLACK
Secretary, Royal and Ancient Golf Club

Golfer holing out on the first green of the Old Course, circa 1880. Notice how the golfer's line to the hole is blocked by his opponent's ball. This was called a 'stymie'. Abolished in 1952 as being an "unfair advantage" and an "embarrassment," the stymie introduced the element of luck or good fortune, unforeseen factors of which the golfer had no control. It had to be accepted in the spirit of the game, maybe with gratitude if yours was the ball obstructing an opponent's line to the hole!

CONTENTS

Caddie Profile: Trap Door

Some caddies had ingenious ways of earning extra money. One such caddie was Willie Johnson, known as 'Trap-Door,' who made a fair amount from 'lost' golf balls. Willie pretended that one leg was shorter than the other and had a special boot made which had a hollow sole, large enough to fit the diameter of a golf ball. During a search in the *whins* or anywhere else, he would work the ball into his hollow boot and declare it lost. The cavity in his boot could hold up to half a dozen golf balls!

INTRODUCTION

The game of golf has traditionally been surrounded by a certain mystique, a distinctive quality which has elevated much of the written material from the strictly prosaic into a more philosophical realm. The caddie has always had a place in that body of lore, usually in apocryphal tales or stories interlaced with fun and humour. I found a typical example some years ago, when I read an article in an old local newspaper dating from the late nineteenth century in which the St. Andrews caddies were described standing sentry-like by the corner of the Old Union Parlour, the forerunner of today's Royal & Ancient Golf Club. Over the years this corner had effectively become their property, and the scene was described thus:

> Consecrated by the fumes of their three-penny cut tobacco wafting in the air, they stand, *blue wi' the cauld* of bleak midwinter or bronze-like with the *gey strang* heat o' midsummer, their fortunes would vary but ever optimistic, and if business was slow, a wee nip at the 19th hole would always warm the inner man.

In truth, until recently the caddie's lot has not been a particularly fortunate one. Although satisfied with their role, in the late nineteenth and early part of the twentieth century they were effectively social outcasts, as caddying was viewed by society in general as 'not a fit and proper job.' In a time of strong class and social distinctions, even local trades people saw themselves as superior to the caddie, who was considered on a par with a street cleaner or a marker in a billiards saloon. Because of the seasonal nature of the work, most lived in a state of poverty. During this period, some members of the R&A took an active interest in their own caddies' welfare by gifting them food and clothing during the hard times when there was no work on the links. With the introduction of the Caddies Benefit Fund in 1891, the Club went to even greater lengths to assure that basic needs were met during the winter months. In spite of this genuine need, the caddies remained a proud and free-spirited band of men, who never lost the hope encompassed in the very motto of St. Andrews itself: *dum spiro spero* (while I breathe, I hope).

My own interest in the history of the St. Andrews caddie developed from some two decades of involvement as a professional caddie both abroad and here at home. The many hours I've spent in libraries, newspaper archives, and in conversation with old-time traditional caddies have given me a glimpse into the lives of some of the characters who spent their days *grasshoppin'* over the links of St. Andrews. One such character, 'Auld Daw' Anderson, was a senior caddie whose *pawky* sense of humour was as legendary as his philosophical wit. He said, "Although devoid of material things, we were rich in courtesy *tae oor* golfers, which in turn made us rich in life."

Over the years, golf has changed from a predominately amateur to a high-profile professional sport. During this time, there has been a corresponding rise in the fortunes of the caddies, who are no longer merely beasts of burden, underpaid and always at the beck and call of the golfer. Today's caddie is a professional whose knowledge and judgement can make an important difference to the golfer with whom he works, and both his remuneration and his status on the links reflect this. During the writing of this book, I have come to appreciate more than ever before the value of the time-honoured tradition of the St. Andrews caddie, a tradition now embodied in the men and women who today *work the land*, still serving the golfer just as colourful characters like Lang Willie, Hole in His Pocket and Stumpie Eye did all those years ago.

Richard Mackenzie
St. Andrews, Scotland

Engraving of golfers on the links of St. Andrews, circa 1880. Notice that the ball is being played two club lengths away from the hole—there is still no defined green. The young caddie, having taken sand from the hole, has prepared a tee for his golfer.

Andrew Greig at the Old Course starter's box, circa 1910. Andrew Greig was the official starter for the Old Course from 1894 until his death in 1915. His starter's box on wheels was a converted Victorian bathing hut, at one time used by lady bathers who swam in the 'gey cauld' waters that surrounded St. Andrews. At a time when the links were rich in personalities, Andrew was one of the most colourful characters. He also had a keen sense of humour. One day he was approached by a Frenchman who asked if he could play the Old Course and gave his name as "Fouquier." "Weel," replied Andrew, "When I cry oot Tamson, jist you step on tae the tee!"

His niece was the first female caddie to work on the links. When she carried in the 1913 Amateur Championship, her golfer had no more than five clubs in his kit, a far cry from some of the heavy golf bags which became fashionable in the mid-thirties.

THE CAWDYS

For hundreds of years the business of carrying clubs has been a way of life for a breed of hardy St. Andreans. Golfers have found that local knowledge of the links goes a long way, and perhaps at no other place is it more true than on the Old Course. Deception is the Old's secret weapon. What can seem like a good drive might finish up amongst the prickly gorse bushes, or land in one of the many hidden pot bunkers. With names like the Coffins, Hell and the infamous Beardies, they lurk out of sight, waiting to trap the unwary. It was said many years ago that when you land in any of those bunkers, "there is only enough room for an angry man and his *niblick*!" *

With acres of gorse bushes, those dreaded bunkers and fairways which flatter to deceive, the caddie is an essential companion and guide. At no other course in the world is the continuity of caddie knowledge handed down from one generation to the next, taking you back in time to the early *pawky* caddie personalities such as Lang Willie, Hole in His Pocket and Stumpie Eye, names that conjure up images of another age. They may be long gone, but the spirit of these men lives on in today's professional caddie. Gone is the complex individual, the perennial thorn in the side of golfers and society alike, who saw himself as a free spirit with a *braw* conceit, for whom no amount of regulation could improve his language or dress sense! Paradoxically, these very men who often lived hand-to-mouth, sometimes sleeping rough in bunkers or wherever they could find shelter, at the same time formed such a fundamental part of the game that the Rules of Golf decree

---

* All italicized Scottish words will be found in the Scottish Glossary at the back of the book.

the caddie to be the only person a player can consult in singles play for advice, and that any infringement of this rule committed by the caddie incurs the same penalty as if committed by the golfer himself.

Sketch of golfers on the St. Andrews links, circa 1700. The Old Union Parlour, precursor to today's Royal & Ancient Golf Club, is the leftmost building in the distance. The Swilcan Burn ran almost the length of the present first and eighteenth fairways. In 1847, Hugh Lyon Playfair, Captain of the R&A and Town Provost, carried out land reclamation and widened this area by building a breakwater to stop the sea encroaching onto the grassy areas during high tide. The reclamation in effect widened the links at this point, and when Tom Morris took over as Keeper of the Green in 1864, he returfed the whole area.

When does the first mention of a caddie appear? The reputed source of the name is given as Mary Queen of Scots. A keen golf enthusiast, she played the game in France where her clubs were carried by young students called "Les Cadets." Such was her passion for the game, she found time to play in the grounds of Seton Palace in East Lothian only a few days after her husband Lord Darnley was murdered in 1567. The earliest mention of the word *caddie* appears in the accounts records of one Andrew Dixon, a ballmaker (1655-1729), who lived near Leith in Edinburgh. He was employed as a fore-caddie by the future King James II, then Duke of York. The name was taken up in the eighteenth century by the male and female water carriers in and around Edinburgh, who were called "Cawdys." This sense of the word indicated a messenger or porter, and early references to the Edinburgh Cawdys described them as "useful blackguards, who attend coffee houses and public places to run errands" and "wretches who lie in streets at night, but were always trusted and never unfaithful." In spite of this, the group was cohesive enough to elect one of their senior members as the Constable of Cawdys, who had virtually complete control over this unique fraternity, with the ability to fine a member or mete out corporal punishment. In those days, as now, caddies had to be registered and issued with a badge before they could ply their trade.

Gentlemen golfers were quick to apply the word to mean 'the man who carries the sticks,' and the boy who ran ahead of the players had become the fore-caddie. The first written evidence of the St. Andrews caddies was recorded on 27 June 1771 in the Minutes of the Society of St. Andrews Golfers, the precursor to today's Royal & Ancient Golf Club. This passage, which expresses the first interest in their welfare, reads:

> The Captains and Company agree and appoint that in time coming, the caddies who carry the clubs, or run before the players, or are otherwise employed by the Gentlemen Golfers, are to get four pence sterling for going the length of the hole called the "Hole O' Cross," and if they go further than that hole they are to get sixpence and no more. Any Gentlemen transgressing this rule are to pay, two pint bottles of Claret, at the first meeting they shall attend.

The course then was not what we know today. It was about half the width and today's seventeenth hole was then the first. The links were originally covered with rough grass, thick gorse and wild heather, and the course was marked out with march stones, with *whin* bushes all the way up the right-hand side of what is the outward part of today's course. Given the undulating land, thick grass and rough ground, it is easy to see why the fore-caddie came into his own at St. Andrews. But the hand of man was already at work. Tom Morris was appointed Keeper of the Green in 1864, after which time he developed a new first and eighteenth green on the Old Course and was involved in widening the fairways. The famous double greens were already in place by the time Tom came from Prestwick. The then-Captain of the R&A, Provost Hugh Lyon Playfair, was instrumental in having the seven double greens cut that St. Andrews is famous for today. These enabled golfers to play either the original left-hand course or the new right-hand one. The right-hand course in time became the accepted one and was used for the first ever Open, played at St. Andrews in 1873.

Thus for over four centuries, the business of carrying golf clubs has been a way of life for this unique and at times perplexing breed, who in all kinds of weather can still be seen lugging their *man's* clubs around the rolling windswept links of St. Andrews. And if the carrying of the clubs is their trade, then knowledge of the courses is their craft, a craft barely understood by the millions of spectators who today follow the sport, either by foot or glued to their television sets.

Over the years the caddie has added richness and colour to this Royal & Ancient game, either in humorous anecdote or in the role played by the early ball- and clubmakers. They cajoled, counselled, inspired and occasionally bullied their *man* around the golf course. David Corstorphine, one of the senior caddies, always offered the same advice before each round: *"Dinna risk awthing, we'll play wi' oor heids."* With this wisdom, it seems such a short step to the caddies giving instruction on how to play, and in time becoming the first professional golfers. Even the caddies who never actually played the game themselves knew the links intimately and were well aware of their *man's* strengths and failings. They saw themselves as a kind of senior partner, who could judge the wind strength, choose the club, and dictate the target area, leaving the simple business of hitting the ball to the player.

Today, the ball- and clubmaking skills may have disappeared, but the good local caddie still has to wait his turn on the daily list and is still in great demand. With over a quarter century of experience in his craft, the St. Andrews caddie can be in his own way a hard and inexorable taskmaster who, from the moment he takes charge of your clubs, assumes the role of the brains of the outfit!

Nineteenth-century engraving of golfers on the Old Course. The R&A Clubhouse, built in 1754, is now prominent on the skyline, and the homes/workshops of Tom Morris and Allan Robertson line the right-hand side of the fairway. Since the links were public land, the townsfolk apparently felt free to stroll around—even within range of the golfers! The caddies are wearing the traditional 'Tam O'Shanter bunnets,' and their golfers are wearing the accepted uniform jackets of the Club.

Caddie Profile: David Corstorphine

Circa 1910. Standing outside the Caddie Superintendent's box under the watchful eye of Caddie Superintendent James Jolly, caddie David Corstorphine has cleaned up his *man's* clubs and awaits the golfer, ready to do battle.

In 1910, new regulations called for caddies to be "tidy in dress, sober when on duty and civil to his man." The caddie was now no longer "free as the fowls o' the air to ply his trade." According to the Town's Greens Committee, they had to come under the influence of the modern demand for regulation.

Caddies and the R&A

After the mid-nineteenth century, local caddies began to be employed on a regular basis by members of the Royal & Ancient Golf Club. There were several good reasons for this, one being the local rule that matches having a caddie in them could play through those which did not. P. G. Tait, a university professor and fanatical golfer, took advantage of this rule. The Professor would play up to six rounds a day, wearing out quite a few caddies in the process. His son, golfing legend Freddie Tait, was a supreme player who in 1895 broke the record for the Old Course with a round of 72. Freddie was seldom seen on the links without his pet dog Nails.

The regular members of the R&A had their own special caddies, and both groups of men added to the character of the links. Club member "Old Sutherland" would have been lost without his trusty caddie Andra' Strath, and both have bunkers on the Old Course named after them. Old Sutherland actually filled in one of the more troublesome of these bunkers late one night with the help of some rebels in the shape of Club members and caddies. The following day the Greens Committee duly reopened it and it is still there today.

Two other R&A members were never seen on the links without their ponies. John Whyte Melville, known as 'Mounty' to the caddies, not only used his pony to ride from his house down to the links but also set off on his round astride his trusty steed, with his breathless caddie trotting fast behind! Mr. Wolfe Murray, one of the older Club members who played golf almost to the end of his days, also used a pony for his rounds. He employed two caddies, one to carry the clubs and one to hold the pony while he got off to play his shot, a practice which led to intense arguments between the caddies about who should have the easier job of holding the pony!

Around this time, local professionals began taking their favourite caddies with them as they moved between courses for tournament play. Allan Robertson always had 'Daw' Anderson, Tom Morris had 'Kirky' and Willie Dun preferred James Wilson, each caddie in his own right an excellent golfer or clubmaker. After play, caddies and players would gather in the local bars and exchange stories, the losers sharing in the entertainment by the generosity of the winners, with the innkeepers getting most of the prize money! This custom still exists amongst the local caddies from the earning of a good week's caddying.

Not all caddies had two legs: painting of R&A member General Sir John Low of Clatto, riding the links at St. Andrews on his faithful cream pony, circa 1870.

Captain in 1865, Sir John played golf well into his 90s, and took to his pony when walking became difficult during the latter part of a round, dismounting between shots. Perhaps droppings left by his trusty steed led to some of the many revisions of Rule 23 (Loose Impediments) which were made by the R&A during the nineteenth century!

Freddie Tait seen in a studio photograph with his pet dog Nails, circa 1895. Freddie broke the Old Course record in that year with a round of 72, and that new record was steadily whittled down until Curtis Strange reduced it to 62 in 1987. Freddie was also the amateur champion in 1896 and 1898. He was admired by all who knew him because of his ready smile and adventurous spirit, but unfortunately golf was to lose a wonderful ambassador at an early age, for Freddie was killed in South Africa while leading his men into action in 1900, age 30. Three lines from Wordsworth's poem The Excursion were chosen for his epitaph:

> *The good die first,*
> *And they whose hearts are dry as summer dust*
> *Burn to the socket. *__

__ Burn to the base of the candlestick.

KEEPER OF THE GREEN

Early R&A records show that the Club attempted to improve the lot of the caddies and at the same time have someone attached to the Club who would both look after its needs and attend to the course. This resulted in the appointment by the R&A of Club Inspectors of the Links, who were authorised to employ one of the senior caddies to take on the duties of what was to become known as the 'Keeper of the Green.' The term 'green' meant all of the golf links, not what we now call the putting surface. These men were instructed to replace any caddie whom they found "inactive or not doing his duty." The first senior caddie to be employed was Geordie Robertson, who some time later, after repeated *wiggings*, was dismissed as incompetent and incorrigible. David Pirie, another caddie, took over from Geordie in 1823. After David came 'Auld Daw' Anderson, one-time ballmaker and caddie who tended the Old Course for many years and then, upon his retirement, set up a ginger beer stall at the ninth hole. Daw was Keeper of the Green until 1855, and he is credited with having cut two holes on the fifth green of the Old Course. Today, it's the fourth hole on the Old Course which is named 'Ginger Beer,' because that's the location where for many years an old woman sold her brew. In very hot weather, thirsty caddies were apt to bypass the stall and drink from a nearby water pump. Discovering this, the woman took away the pump handle, an act which sparked an ongoing battle between herself and the caddies for the next several years. Sadly, there are no records to show the outcome.

In 1856, after the retirement of 'Auld Daw,' the R&A promoted two caddies, Watty Alexander and Alex Herd, as Keepers of the Green at a joint wage of £6 per year. When extra help was required, local pensioners, who affectionately came to be known as "rabbits," were taken on to cut the holes and sweep rabbit droppings from the greens. These men had no special knowledge of course management, and had only barrows, a couple of shovels, and brushes to work with, a far cry from today's professional greenkeepers. Tom Morris took over as Keeper of the Green in 1863, at a considerably increased salary of £50 per year, plus the help of one additional man during medal weeks.

Greens staff up to their knees in silt doing running repairs on the Old Course prior to the Walker Cup, 1934.

Eddie Adams, Head Greenkeeper for the Old Course since 1990. Just as Tom Morris redesigned the layout of the Old Course prior to the first Open in 1873, so Eddie is supervising the preparation of the course prior to the Millennium Open. Although his job is technically more advanced than in years gone by, the basic principles have remained the same since the days of Old Tom. Beach sand is still used on the course as a top dressing, and bunker sand, fertilizer and water are used in minimal amounts.

The administrative and communication skills required for today's greenkeeper have elevated him/her to the status of a professional manager, as well as promoting the art of greenkeeping as a possible career choice. It's a far cry from Geordie Robertson's 'repeated wiggings'!

Above: Early twentieth century tournament. Crowd control was not a major consideration here—the golfers seem to be lost in a maze of Victorian headwear. The canopies on both sides of the R&A Club windows are no longer there, and the old Victorian 'bathing hut' has now been replaced by today's modern starter's box.

Facing page: By 1865, a set of rules including pay and discipline were proposed, printed and posted in the Clubhouse. By then, Tom Morris had become Keeper of the Green at a salary of £50 per year. Apparently, there was cause for the Club to address the issue of intemperance even in the Boy Caddies.

The ground appears to have been prepared for either Morris, Forgan or Wilson to eventually take over the duties of Caddie Superintendent. Since both Forgan and Wilson preferred the work bench to the golf course, the field was left open to Tom Morris.

Rules and Discipline of Caddies ~ 1864

1. No Boy under Eleven years of age shall be admitted as a Caddie.

2. Boys admitted as Caddies shall be required to continue their Education and also to attend a Sunday School.

3. Swearing, intemperance, dishonesty and the use of improper or uncivil language shall be strictly prohibited at all times on pain of dismissal.

4. All Boys admitted as Caddies shall be provided with a Cap, bearing the Club Badge which he must wear on the Links, so long as he is to be employed, and return to the Club, when he retires or is dismissed.

5. No Boy who engages himself to a Gentleman in the morning shall be allowed to break that engagement till the day's play is over, or if he does, shall forfeit half his forenoon's pay.

6. All Caddie Boys shall consider themselves as Boys till they reach the age of Eighteen years.

7. Messrs. Morris, Forgan, Wilson, and the Club Steward shall be appointed to fix upon the proper Boys to select as Caddies, to take a supervision of them, and to receive any complaints that have to be made and these to be remitted to the Green Committee for adjudication, and they having full power in this matter their sentence shall be final.

8. All Boys admitted as Caddies in the service shall have a copy of these Rules given them, and in the event of any contravention of them, the guilty party will be liable to suspension if not expulsion from the service.

Below: R&A member James Balfour is about to tee off with young Jamie Anderson (later a three-time winner of the Open Championship) amongst a group of caddies and golfers, circa 1855. The cottage in the background is the present-day Jigger Inn, then part of the old railway station which was shortly afterwards moved into the town. The relocation made the station more convenient to shops and also solved the problem of passengers disembarking onto the golf course and interrupting play!

Facing page: rules poster, 1875.

First Class caddies were valued not only for their experience, but their sobriety and conduct on the golf course. Good caddies were expected to make sand tees to the golfer's requirements, and the clever caddie, after completing the tee, would moisten the ball with a well-licked thumb before placing it on top, thereby insuring that some grains of sand stuck to it and created some helpful back spin for his golfer! The caddie would offer advice tailored to his golfer's strengths and weaknesses, club him, and give him lines off the tee and on the green. At the end of the round, he would clean and oil the clubs, lightly rubbing the heads with a fine piece of emery paper, and return them to the Clubhouse where he would be paid his fee.

Second Class caddies were altogether a different breed. Even though some were just as experienced as the more senior caddies, they were less dependable, often drunk, and would at times show no consideration for their golfer. So much was the image of a typical caddie linked with drink that a level of drunkenness was often tolerated which would have seen the 'rogue' out of work in any other job.

RULES

REGARDING

PAY AND DISCIPLINE OF CADDIES,

ADOPTED BY

THE ROYAL AND ANCIENT GOLF CLUB OF ST. ANDREWS,

At a Special General Meeting of the Club, held on 3rd February, 1875.

I.—All Caddies shall be Enrolled,—none being admitted under 13 years of age.

II.—Members of the Club shall employ only Enrolled Caddies.

III.—A List of Enrolled Caddies shall be placed in the Club Hall, and also in the Clubmakers' Shops.

IV.—Caddies shall be divided into Two Classes, according to skill or age, and their services shall be rated as follows:—

First Class Caddies,—Eighteenpence for First Round, and One Shilling for each following Round, or part of Round.

Second Class Caddies,—One Shilling for First Round, and Sixpence for each following Round, or part of Round.

V.—No Caddy, unless previously engaged, can refuse to carry for a Member, under penalty of suspension for a stated time.

VI.—Names of suspended or disqualified Caddies shall be posted.

VII.—Complaints regarding Caddies shall be made through the Keeper of the Green to the Green Committee, who shall award an adequate penalty.

VIII.—The penalty shall be awarded by not less than two of the Green Committee.

IX.—The Keeper of the Green shall have charge of the Caddies, and Members shall apply to him when in want of a Caddy.

X.—Members are particularly urged to report all cases of misconduct on the part of the Caddies, whether during their time of service or otherwise,—such as incivility, bad language, abusing the Green, or any other form of misdemeanour,—which may merit censure or penalty.

XI.—Tom Morris shall be Keeper of the Green, and Superintendent of the Caddies.

THE FLEESING SHEDS

For those mid-nineteenth-century caddies not fortunate enough to be tied to a professional golfer, there arose the need for a set of standard regulations to guard both the caddies and the public. Beginning in 1860, several attempts were made by the R&A to grapple with the regulations governing the employment of caddies, but it was four years before R&A member Major Boothby submitted to the Club a list of caddies to be employed and a set of regulations for their employment. Up to the age of eighteen, 'Boy Caddies' had to continue their education, attend Sunday School and refrain from using bad language picked up from the older caddies. Now all caddies were to be supplied with a cap sporting the Club badge which they had to wear while on the links, and no caddie was allowed on the links who was not on the list.

By 1870, the R&A introduced a further set of rules and regulations, an "interference" to which the caddies reacted by staging a strike for higher wages. A local newspaper stated that "broken down artisans interfered with the rights of the hereditary caddie. Now times have changed and communism has leavened the noble mind." Strong words indeed, but in reality, the caddie's only concern was for the change in his pocket, not a change of times!

Although many of the Club members were sympathetic to the caddies' cause, their action was unsuccessful, because they did not win an increase in the rate. Caddie rates for first class caddies were set at 1/6d* for the first round and 6d for the second or part thereof.

---

* The British monetary system was changed to decimal currency in 1971. In the old system, one shilling, written as 1/-, would equal 5 new pence in today's

Second class caddies were paid 1/- and 6d for the second round. The recognised tip was 1/-, which most R&A members paid after all the golf clubs had been cleaned. These rates remained the same for many years to come. However, a positive result for both parties was the appointment by the R&A of the Keeper of the Green Tom Morris as the first Caddie Superintendent, with full authority over the striking caddies. It was expected that Tom would be sympathetic with the caddies while also understanding the needs of Club members.

The problem of regulating caddies was not peculiar to St. Andrews. During the next thirty years, nearly thirty of the leading golf clubs throughout Britain requested guidance in this matter from the R&A, seeking standardised rules for caddies. For example, in both Musselburgh and St. Andrews, visitors were being charged exorbitant rates by the caddies, and the caddie shacks were described as "Fleesing Sheds." Both links were public land, so no tariff control could guard against the caddie hell-bent on fleecing the unsuspecting golfer. As the local press observed,

> many remember the manner in which the guileless golfer was pounced upon by hordes of Raggamuffins at St. Andrews Railway station, their battle cry being, 'Carry for you sir, carry for you, sir.' The golfer would surrender, as it were, body and soul, being *deaved* out of all his wits by the incessant clamour, how ultimately in too many cases, he was unconsciously parted from his money.

As a result of these ongoing problems, the R&A Greens Committee established a Register of Authorised Caddies in 1891, along with new stricter provisions for the control of caddies. New regulations, which

---

currency. An old penny, written as 1d, would equal about 1/2 new pence. The rate of one shilling and six pennies (1/6d), which the caddie would pronounce "one and six," would amount to 7 new pence.

included both local Club rules dealing with dress and behaviour and bye-laws covering the employment of caddies, stipulated that "no person should act as a caddie for hire until licensed by the Town Magistrates" and also determined the tariff payable to the caddies, with each caddie agreeing "that the conditions and regulations shall be observed." A licensed caddie could not refuse any engagement with a Club member, and while on the links he had to wear an officially numbered badge, now a rather cumbersome brass plate mounted on a leather armband. To ensure the impartial meting-out of justice, the responsibility for enforcement was now handed to the Town Council, and those who tried to work the links without being registered were brought before the local court. Those arrested and charged with breaking the bye-laws would appear before the magistrate and be given a severe *wigging* with no right of appeal. Justice being summary, if they persisted in 'bootlegging' they would receive "a penalty not exceeding 10/- or seven days imprisonment, and suspension or revocation of his caddie licence." Caddies who broke the Club rules were also faced with the threat of suspension.

Caddie arm badge which all registered caddies were required to wear from 1891 until replaced by the cap and badge.

To enforce these new regulations and to take the first step in formally distancing the Club committees from the day-to-day handling of the caddies, the R&A looked for a man who could take over caddie-related record-keeping and who could employ the needed diplomacy with greater authority than Tom Morris, who after all had started as a caddie himself in St. Andrews and personally knew most of those under his wing. Tom Morris was truly legendary, and one of the great architects of golf history, but this good man took the caddies' interest too much to heart, and thus was unable to enforce the level of authority now required by the R&A. That same year, the Club found the desired combination of administrator, diplomat and disciplinarian in Royal Navy retiree Nicholas Robb, whom they appointed to the position of R&A Club Officer, with the combined duties of Hall Porter, Caddie Superintendent, and Secretary of the newly-established Caddies Benefit Fund, at an annual salary of £60 paid out of Club funds.

Robb's role as Hall Porter made it essential that he be stationed within the Clubhouse. Business of the day was done at a small desk in the hall, where payment to caddies was made after each round. This was also where each caddie would pay a deposit of 2/6d * to Robb at the beginning of the season. He would then issue the caddie with a badge and put his name on the caddie list for that year, which would be displayed in the Clubhouse and in the local clubmakers' shops. By 1912, Nicholas Robb's title had become Caddie Master at St. Andrews.

Nicholas Robb's appointment was initially seen by the caddies as a threat to a comfortable status quo. According to the Greens Committee minutes, the caddies resisted vehemently but were eventually won over by Mr. Robb, who convinced them that the Club was acting on their behalf by "insuring regularity and impartiality of employment to all of the registered caddies." In spite of the caddies' early reaction and the resultant negative publicity in the local press, the caddies still had the interest of the golfer at heart, and it was also

---

* Two shillings and 6 pennies (2/6d) would have been pronounced by the caddies as "*twa* and six," and would equal about 12 new pence.

reported that it was "unfair to think of them as reckless, couldn't-care-less types, with nothing but money and ale in their heads." At the end of the day, the winning of the match was as important to the caddie as it was to the golfer.

Group of caddies, circa 1910. In spite of so much negative publicity, it was still said of the caddies that it was "unfair to think of them as reckless, couldn't-care-less types, with nothing but money and ale in their heads." The golfer and caddie had a mutual respect for each other, and they shared a common goal: the winning of the match.

Caddie Profile: Tom Morris

Tom Morris' early years were spent as a caddie working the links at St. Andrews. The son of a hand-loom weaver, his skills as a golfer and clubmaker led to him being appointed the Professional at Prestwick. Tom is considered one of the greatest St. Andrews golfers, winning the Championship Belt (the precursor to the Open Championship) in 1861 and 1862 while still at Prestwick, and in 1864 and 1867 after returning to his native St. Andrews.

In 1864, the Royal & Ancient Golf Club decided to appoint someone who would not only take charge of the course management, but would serve as the Honorary Professional to the Club as well. Since Allan Robertson had died in 1859, the only suitable candidate was Tom Morris. Although Old Tom was currently at Prestwick, the St. Andrews native was persuaded to return to his home town and take over the Club duties. He set up business in what had been a 'Sweetie' shop near the Rusacks Hotel, then later moved up the road to the shop opposite the eighteenth green which still bears his name. Here he combined the duties of clubmaker, greenkeeper and Caddie Superintendent. Caddies were now expected to appear for work clean and moderately sober, and Tom inspected them daily—sometimes a singularly unrewarding experience!

With Tom Morris' appointment came the laying down of a new last green on the Old Course. The original finishing hole was in front of the depression known as the 'Valley of Sin.' The area in those days was a much larger hole which was filled in to its present level to constitute the now famous eighteenth at St. Andrews, a compliment to Tom's greenkeeping skills.

Nicholas Robb

Nicholas Robb, who had served 23 years in the Royal Navy, acted as the R&A Hall Porter, and assisted the Greens Committee and the Secretary on medal days. He also assisted members with their clubs and boxes, and issued members with their clubs, ready to be cleaned by the caddies.

Fifteen pounds of Nicholas Robb's annual salary was taken from the Caddie Benefit Fund in the form of a grant, but by 1895, there were insufficient funds to cover this levy, and it was agreed to discontinue payment to Mr. Robb in this form.

CADDIES BENEFIT FUND

Upon his appointment as Officer of the Club in 1891, one of Nicholas Robb's duties was acting as Secretary of the newly-formed Caddies Benefit Fund. This Fund was established by the R&A for the relief of caddies and professional golfers who from old age, illness, accident or other unavoidable cause were incapable of regular work. It also gave temporary assistance to the widows and children of caddies or professional golfers who had been left destitute. Caddies were asked to subscribe to the Fund at the rate of two pence per week from 1st October to 30th June, and 4d per week during July, August and September. This amount was paid to Nicholas Robb each Saturday, but in the event that a caddie could not pay regularly for lack of work on the links or for any other satisfactory reason, his contributions could be deferred with the agreement of the committee. A caddie could also pay his contribution in advance. Mr. Robb was responsible for the weekly dues collection, while Tom Morris and two other professionals were appointed to represent the 'paid ranks' on the R&A Management Committee which controlled the Fund and administered benefits.

In addition to the caddies' contributions, the Fund was supplemented by an annual grant that was set by the R&A, donations and subscriptions from members and other locals, and a percentage of monies taken from Club sweepstakes. This was an important step in the R&A's concern for the caddies' welfare, and reflected the philanthropic attitudes of the Victorian period. Caddies (and their families) received such things as coal and groceries upon presenting a written certificate that they were unable to work on the links. In 1892, twenty-one caddies received assistance from the Fund and three men had their contributions returned when their registrations were withdrawn. In some cases, the caddie's hospital bills were paid from the Fund, and funeral expenses were paid to the families of those caddies who died.

In spite of these good works, by 1895 the Caddies Benefit Fund had virtually petered out because most caddies became increasingly unwilling to part with their hard-earned money. In those difficult times, the penny in the pocket had far more weight than the pound in the ledger for these men used to a hand-to-mouth existence.

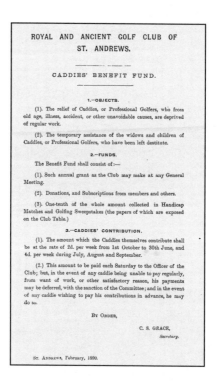

Poster of the Caddies Benefit Fund, circa 1890.

Caddie Register, 1894. Andra' Kirkaldy decided to withdraw his registration as a caddie this year, feeling that he could not both caddie and work as a professional golfer. Some other caddies' registrations were withdrawn for non-payment to the Caddies Benefit Fund, but the benefits to caddies and their families can clearly be seen, with assistance given to cover funeral expenses.

List of Caddies Names who has received
Assistance from the Fund during Sickness
For the past year

1892

	Names	Amount £ S d
Feb 12	Arthur Fenton for 6 weeks at 6/ per week	15
" 24	John Lee not on the Fund then	2
March 9	William Wilson " "	5
" 16	William Wilson " "	5
" 28	William Wilson " "	5
April 7	William Wilson " "	5
June 13	James Eddie " "	5
July 26	Pd to Cottage Hospital per J. McGregor for 2 weeks	10
August 9	James Lister " "	5
Oct 19	Arthur Fenton " "	5
" 24	Arthur Fenton " "	5
" 31	Arthur Fenton "	5
Nov	Arthur Fenton " "	5
" 14	William Thomson " "	5
" 14	Arthur Fenton " "	5
" 19	William Thomson " "	2 " 6
" 19	Arthur Fenton " "	5
" 29	David Cuthbert " "	2 " 6
Dec 27	John Herd " "	5
" 27	James Lister " "	5
1893 Jan 10	Pd to Mr Kinnaith for Medicine Supplied	
" "	to D. Cuthbert and J. McGregor "	5 " 11 ½
" 14	William Wilson " "	5
" 21	John Lee	2 " 6
Feb 22	Pd to Cottage Hospital for J. Lee for 4½ weeks in Hospital at 6/ per week "	1 2 " 6
"	Pd to Arthur Fenton from His Contribution for the Funeral expenses of His daughter	£7 2 " 11 ½
		10
		£7 12 " 11 ½

Nicholas Ross

List of caddies who received assistance, 1892.

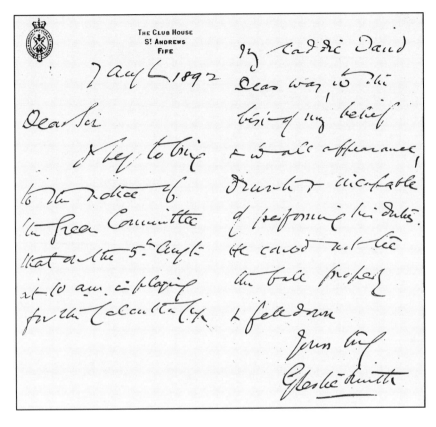

Letter of complaint from R&A member G. Leslie Smith, 1892. The text reads:

Dear Sir,
I beg to bring to the notice of the Green Committee that on the 5th of August at 10 am, in playing for the Calcutta Cup, my caddie, David Deas, was, to the best of my belief and to all appearance, drunk and incapable of performing his duties. He could not tee the ball properly and fell down.

Yours truly,
G. Leslie Smith

Mention is also made in the 1893 Caddie Committee minutes of caddie David Gourlay, who in his latter years used his bicycle to carry clubs around the Old Course. He was fined in the local magistrate's court, not for using his bicycle, but for being drunk and cycling without a rear light!

Caddie Offences, 1891. Even with all the assistance and consideration given to the caddies by the Club, some individuals still felt the need to express themselves either through drink or disrespect. Unfortunately, in most cases this was practised on the golf course, and as a result, some of the caddies mentioned in the Register were severely reprimanded, and for those caddies who could not adjust to the required standards, had their licences withdrawn.

REGISTER

Offences

No.	NAME.	DATE OF REGISTRY.	
1892		Hall Depn &c	
		By Committee	
February 11th	John Kirk was under the influence of Drink on the above date and did use threatening Language to Mr. Lee a Member of the Club	Suspended for 14 days By Order 15.2.92	(1)
	John Kirk		
April 18th	Reported by Mr. J. Smart for being drunk. And refusing to carry his Clubs After being engaged by him to do so	21st April — Suspended from duty for 1 Month. By Order —	(2)
June 24.	John Kirk. Drunk at the door of the Club House and making use of foul language towards Dr. Blackwell.	27th June Name Removed from List by Green Committee.	(3). Suspended for 10 days from date of offence R&A H—
May 8	John Ferguson reported by Mr Blackwell for being Drunk And unfit to go out with Mr Cathcart	Suspended for One week	

Caddie Offences, 1892.

THE DOG LICENCE

By 1920, the original Caddies Benefit Fund had long since been stopped and patronage of the R&A was diminishing in the wake of the First World War. But some members of the Club were still sensitive to the financial hardship posed for some of the men during the months of December and January when there was little or no work on the links. Some of the older, traditional caddies whose livelihood depended on their seasonal earnings on the links were employed during the winter months as *ghillies* during shoots on nearby estates, and a discretionary, non-contributory fund was introduced for them.

Under the provisions of this new Caddies Benefit Fund, these men were given a voucher for 7/6d which could be exchanged for groceries at most local shops. The caddies referred to the voucher as the 'Dog Licence' since 7/6d was the cost of a licence to own a dog. Some of the better caddies, regardless of age, were also placed on the voucher list. When exchanging the voucher, the caddie badge had to be shown before any goods could be purchased. Some caddies would exchange their badges for the 2/6d deposit after the voucher was gone, but would have to find the money again to ensure their place on the caddie list for the new season. Several of the local pubs were quick to offer the caddies inducements to have the vouchers cashed with them. On one occasion, five pints of beer were offered in exchange for the caddie voucher, a temptation some probably found hard to ignore!

Caddie Profile: Stuart Rodger

As of this writing, there is only one recipient of this new Caddies Benefit Fund alive, Stuart Rodger, now 85. Stuart began caddying when a schoolboy of 13 and worked on the links on and off until he retired in 1975. He was caddie to many fine golfers, but is remembered for his reply when he worked for the former Prime Minister Harold Macmillan. After the round, he was asked by reporters what he thought of Mr Macmillan's golf. He replied, "He's a fine gentleman, but he's nothing but a part-time golfer." Those nearby criticised Stuart for his impoliteness but he defended himself by declaring, "I should know, I'm *wan* myself."

> Valid for the the period 15th Dec. 1994
> to 15th Jan. 1995, only   St. Andrews, 9/1/95
>
> Please supply *STEWART RODGER* with groceries to the value of *FIFTY POUNDS* and charge same to the Caddies Benefit Fund.
>
> Merchants' accounts must be submitted by the 31st January .
>
> Treasurer,
> Caddies Benefit Fund.
> Royal & Ancient Golf Club of St. Andrews.

Fund voucher for Stuart Roger, 1995. Stuart's retirement is made easier by this annual gift from R&A Club funds.

Top: Caddie Application, 1894. Subscription to the Caddies Benefit Fund was included in the benefits, but only on condition of receiving the "promised annual bonus."

Bottom: Caddies Benefit Fund voucher, on behalf of caddie David Corstorphine, to a local merchant for bag of coal, 1891.

EDUCATION

Nineteenth-century R&A patronage of the caddies extended into the realm of education. In the early 1870s, R&A member General Moncrieffe decided on a plan to encourage the younger caddies, who would rather earn ninepence or a shilling by carrying a 'bag of sticks' for the golfer than attend school, to learn to read. A rhyme of the period told the story:

> Caddying a' the day
> Daein' nae wark at a'
> Runnin' aboot wi' a wee bag o' sticks
> Efter a wee bit ba'! *

A wooden board was put up around the base of the Club flagpole and the ladies of the town gave the caddies 'coffee and instruction.' Unfortunately, large quantities of coffee led to the outdoor "reading room" being used for an "ignoble purpose," and the instruction became useless when the coffee was stopped! Then in 1873 a Greens Committee was introduced. Apart from keeping discipline, its duty was to liaise with the School Board on the matter of evening classes for the caddies.

Consecrated by the fumes of his threepenny cut tobacco, caddie John Lorrie prepares to oil his 'man's' clubs prior to a round.

In the background can be seen the base of the flagpole where the "reading room" was sited.

---

* Caddying all the day, doing no work at all, running about with a small bag of sticks, after a tiny ball!

In 1875, General Moncrieffe, now Town Provost, introduced formal evening classes for all the registered 'Boy Caddies.' They were held in the Fishers School opposite the Cathedral. Around 30 caddies enrolled for the first lessons, and the best reader and best writer at the end of term were each given 12/-, while the best attendee received 10/-. Even good comportment paid, as the best behaved caddie got an additional 8/-. The catch was that no money was ever handed over to the caddie. Instead, each winner's amount was credited to his 'clothing fund,' controlled by Mr. Forgan the clubmaker.

Older caddies were also encouraged to learn to read. By 1883, the R&A had given a yearly subscription of £50 and sent their day-old newspapers to a workingmen's coffee house near the harbour. The caddies were encouraged to use the Fisherman's Coffee House, and for a time there were some who took advantage of the R&A's kindness. 'College' was the nickname given to one caddie who boasted that after many months in the 'reading room' he was college taught. The coffee house was eventually sold, and it was decided that a proper Caddie Shelter should be erected behind the eighteenth green on the Old Course.

The caddie shelter, for use during wet or snowy weather, was built in 1891. It was sited opposite the main door of the R&A Clubhouse at the location of the present car park, was partially furnished, and had a stove installed. The caddies were supplied with newspapers and a small library. Rules were drawn up for the use of the shelter and the library, and a Vigilance Committee, headed by Tom Morris, was appointed by the caddies themselves to maintain order and discipline within the caddie ranks. On a particularly wet and windy day, one of the older caddies was in the library while waiting for work. He had a book on his knee and was ostensibly reading it, but a lad who knew he couldn't read told him, "The book's the wrong way up!" To this, the senior caddie replied, "Any fool can read a book the *richt* way up. It takes a good man *tae* read it upside *doon*!!"

Additionally, the Greens Committee introduced a revised system of payment as a form of security. The registered caddies who were on the list had to pay a 2/6d deposit at the start of the season. At the end of the year, after any damage done to the Caddie Shelter had been paid for, the Club doubled the money left over and the whole sum was divided amongst those caddies who had gone through the year with a 'clean sheet.' Clothing was provided for needy caddies out of a special fund, especially during the winter months when little or no work was to be found on the links. Golfers would also pass on any surplus clothes to their caddies. Both parties accepted this as normal, with no hint of embarrassment on either side. Indeed, one caddie boasted to his *man* about his close friendship with Mr. Balfour, a former Prime Minister. When this was received with some incredulity, the caddie indignantly snorted, "I should *ken* him *wel* and I *dae*, I'm wearin' a pair o' his *breeks*."

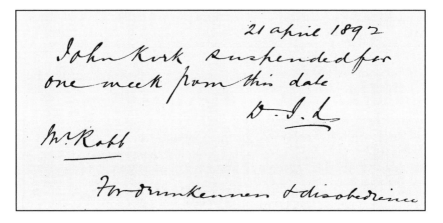

Suspension of caddie for "drunkenness and disobedience," 1892.

THE BETTER HOLE

Although officially-sanctioned assistance to the caddies from the R&A had stopped by the 1920s, the members' personal interest in their caddies did not diminish. In 1938, Mr. Blackwell, past Captain of the R&A, treated the caddies to a New Year's dinner in the 19th Hole Hotel opposite the eighteenth green of the Old Course, more commonly known by the caddies as the 'Better Hole.' At the dinner, every caddie was given a 12/- voucher for groceries, and the happy caddies, once *fu' o' ale*, often broke into song. Among the most vociferous were Jock Hutchison and Jimmy Ferguson, whose famous *Doo-Dah verses* were enjoyed by everyone. Mrs. Blackwell continued this traditional 'do' for some years after her husband's death, but was forced to temporarily suspend it during the war years.

January 1947 saw the return of the caddies' dinner, this time hosted by Mr. Blackwell's son. Even with the post-war rationing, a hearty meal was enjoyed by all, and the caddies were again recorded as being in fine voice. The Caddie Master 'Wingy' Radley thanked Blackwell's son on behalf of all the caddies.

Sign outside Caddie Shelter, circa 1950. Tips had now become discretionary, since caddies no longer had to 'rub up' their 'man's' clubs. Gratuities were now earned on the golf course.

Caddie Fees

The caddie fee is entirely in the discretion of the player.

It is recommended that it should not exceed 30/- per round plus tip if warranted.

Joint Links Committee St. Andrews

Caddie register for St. Andrews, circa 1870. Three Open Championship winners are included in this list, Willie Fernie (1893), Thomas Kidd, Jr. (1873), and Robert Martin (1876, 1885).

Also on the list were some local characters and some very fine golfers who never won an Open Championship but figured in tournaments and big-money matches. John Thompson was known as the 'weather man'. James 'Skipper' Fenton gave up his fishing trawler for the links. David 'Wiggy' Ayton was never seen on the links without his wig and bunnet securely fixed on his head! Walter 'Watty' Alexander took over as Caddie Superintendent when Tom Morris was off playing in tournaments or the money matches often arranged between players and R&A Club members.

Royal and Ancient Golf Club,
ST ANDREWS.

Caddies Library 1894

1. Any registered caddie may read the books in the "Caddies Library," while he is in the Shelter; receiving the book he wishes from the Club Officer and returning it to him, when he is done with it.

2. Any registered caddie may receive one volume at a time from the Club Officer and take it home for a period of not longer than one week, returning it thereafter to the Club Officer.

3. Any caddie who injures a book belonging to the library or fails to return it, shall have his name removed from the List of Registered Caddies.

By order of the Committee

William Knight

N.B. Any registered Caddie convicted of begging from members of the Club or others, is liable to have his name removed from the Registered List.

By order of the Committee

CADDIES. REGISTER

No.	NAME.	DATE OF REGISTRY.
Nº 1	David Corstorphine	Feb. 2ᵈ 1891
„ 2	James Fenton - jun -	„
„ 3	Robert Lewis	„
„ 4	John Fleak	„
„ 5	James Lawton	„
„ 6	William Wilson	„
„ 7	Alexander Taylor	Feb. 3ᵈ 1891
„ 8	Robert Kinsman	„
„ 9	John Riddle	„
„ 10	Arthur Fenton Son	„
„ 11	John Herd	„
„ 12	James Kinsman	„
„ 13	Chas. Quchterlonie	„
„ 14	John Ferguson	„
„ 15	George Wilson	„
„ 16	John Kirk	„
„ 17	James Arbuthnot	Feb. 4ᵗʰ 1891
„ 18	David Kirkaldy	„
„ 19	James Balmer	„
„ 20	Andrew Kirkaldy	„
„ 21	David Culbert	„
„ 22	Robert Wilson	„
„ 23	William Russel	„
„ 24	John Kirkaldy	„
„ 25	Andrew Traill	Feb. 4ᵗʰ 91
„ 26	John Lees	Feb. 5ᵗʰ 91
„ 27	William Oyston	„
„ 28	David Oyston	„
„ 29	James Robertson	„
„ 30	William Mathews	„

Caddies Register, 1891. Many men who later went on to make a name for themselves as professional golfers or in the administration of the links got their start as caddies. Andra' Kirkaldy came off the register in 1891 when he became a professional golfer. Alexander 'Wingy' Taylor and David Corstorphine graduated from the ranks of the caddies to become Caddie Masters. John Kirk, known as 'Kirky,' became a ballmaker of repute, and was famous for his guttie remakes called 'Kirky's remakes.'

Caddie Profile: ' Poot' Chisholm

" Wi guid porritch and a wee nip, yer a' richt for life."

When asked about the secret of his long life, 'Poot' was heard to say, *" Wi guid porritch and a wee nip, yer a' richt for life."** He was a somewhat disreputably-dressed caddie, and when shown this photograph of himself, he looked at it carefully and then proceeded to ask repeatedly whether it was really of him. After being reassured that it was, 'Poot' gravely said, *"Och* man, it's such a *humblin' sicht."*

* With good porridge and a wee nip, you're all right for life.

The Captain's Dilemma

One of the most famous rituals of the R&A Golf Club is the annual driving-in ceremony by the incoming captain. It takes place at 8am (known as the hangman's hour!) on the last morning of the Club's Autumn Meeting. With one stroke, accompanied by the ceremonial firing of the cannon (the first cannon used was bought for £2 in 1837 from a Prussian Captain, but replaced in 1892 by the one still in use today), the Captain Elect will drive himself into office. On that morning, 20-30 caddies will be standing about in the cold morning air, all waiting expectantly at varying distances down the first fairway. Ever alert and cynical, the caddies by now know the Captain's game, and the unfortunate Captain-Elect who has a habitual slice will feel less confident about his tee shot when he sees a line of caddies all standing by the out-of-bounds fence on the right! As the clock strikes the hour, the caddies all jostle for position, the cannon and drive go off simultaneously and the 'scramble for the ba" is now on, each caddie anxious to retrieve the ball and receive the traditional gold sovereign as a reward.

Right: The first post-war playing-in ceremony was for R&A Captain Roger Wethered in 1946. Since the traditional sovereign was unavailable, the successful caddie, David Herd, proudly displays the £1 note he received.

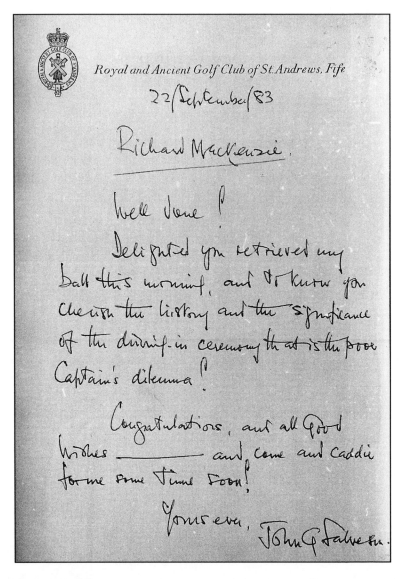

Royal and Ancient Golf Club of St. Andrews, Fife

22 September 83

Richard MacKenzie.

Well done!

Delighted you retrieved my ball this morning, and to know you checked the history and the significance of the driving-in ceremony that is the poor Captain's dilemma!

Congratulations, and all Good Wishes ———— and come and caddie for me some time soon!

Yours ever,
John G Salvesen.

The author has joined the long list of successful caddies in retrieving the Captain's ball. The year caddies became part of the ceremony, and the name of the first caddie to return the captain's ball, are not recorded, though the first playing-in of the Captain-Elect, Sir John Whyte Melville, was in 1823. Previously, the winner of the Silver Club automatically became Captain. It may be assumed that the caddies' role in the ceremony began sometime after 1824.

THE CADDIES' CRAFT

AULD DAVIE

The earliest recorded St. Andrews caddie was David Robertson. Davie, father of the immortal Allan Robertson, is mentioned in a verse of George Carnegie's famous poem *Golfiana*, published in 1833. It reads:

> Davie, oldest of the Cads
> Who gives half-one to unsuspicious lads
> When he might give them two or even more
> and win, perhaps, three matches out of four!!

A reference in the same poem makes it quite clear that Davie, being a senior caddie, was in great demand as a player and teacher.

In Auld Davie's time, the status of professional had not yet been invented. Although there were some Clubs which offered a special position to senior caddies called Officer to the Club, the men employed were still no more than uniformed caddies, whose duty was to carry the clubs of the Captain and run before him to announce where his ball fell. Auld Davie performed the duty of what was then called the Fore-caddie, a title which is the origin of today's cry 'Fore!', still used to inform those ahead to take care.

David Robertson died in 1836, and Carnegie eulogised him in verse:

> Great Davie Robertson the eldest Cad
> in whom the good was stronger than the bad
> he sleeps in death, and with him sleeps his skill
> Which Davie, Statesman-like could wield at will.

'Skipper' Stewart Fenton, circa 1890. Stewart typifies the late nineteenth-century fisherman/ caddie. The fishermen, or 'foreigners' as they were known to the traditional caddies, initially may have seemed like 'fish out of water,' but they took to the links with such enthusiasm that eventually their caddying skills and golfing abilities won them acceptance, and in time, their fisherman's garb became the standard form of attire. Some of them, like Skipper, not only knew the game intimately but played a good game as well.

REGULATIONS FOR THE EMPLOY-MENT OF CADDIES.

A Register of Caddies, in alphabetical order, approved of by the Committee, will be found in the Club-House, and Members, in accordance with the Resolution of the Club at the General Meeting in September 1890, are required to select their Caddies from it.

(If no particular selection be made the Caddies are to be employed in the order of the Register.)

If at any time it be found necessary to have an additional temporary Register of Caddies, the permanent one must be exhausted before the supplementary is resorted to.

TARIFF FOR CADDIES :—

(1.) During the months of July, August, and September, } 1s 6d for each round or part of a round.

(2.) During the rest of year, } 1s 6d for 1st round or part of a round, 1s for each subsequent round or part of a round.

N.B.—The Spring and Autumn meeting weeks are excepted from the above.

(3.) During the Spring and Autumn Meeting weeks, exclusive of the Medal Round, } 2s for each round or part of a round.

(4.) For the Medal Round, - - - 5s.

(5.) For whole Medal Week, inclusive of the Medal Round, } 25s.

TARIFF for PROFESSIONALS : — Playing with a Member, 2s 6d for each round or part of a round, and his Caddie's fee. Teaching a Member, 2s 6d for each round or part of a round.

Members may make special arrangements for lengthened periods with Registered Caddies, provided the Club Tariff be not exceeded.

The Committee reserve power to suspend a Registered Caddie for misconduct for a period to be determined by them, and in grave cases to remove a Caddie's name from the Register.

Note.—In all probability there will be a fund of from £50 to £75 per annum at the disposal of the Committee for the assistance of Registered Caddies, in case of need. Caddies registered before the 14th February 1891 will have a prior claim to the benefits of this fund, which will be administered by Rules hereafter to be framed.

Caddies who wish to have their names placed on the Register must apply to Tom Morris.

Caddie Regulations, 1890. Summer and winter rates for caddies are now set at different tariffs, and the professional or teaching caddie is now distinguished by a separate (and higher) rate structure. The 1875 Regulations were still in effect.

Consideration was now given to a fund for registered caddies whereby the Club contributed £50-£75 per annum for assistance in times of need. This was the start of the Caddies Benefit Fund.

Alex Brown, known as 'Pint Size,' circa 1890. Pint Size's tidy dress shows early influence from the fishermen/caddies' smart attire.

Caddie Profile: Sandy Pirie

"instruments of war"

Sandy operated with the idea that no one could ever beat his *man*, and always referred to the clubs as "instruments of war." He would always carry the clubs in his left hand, rather than the time-honoured method of carrying them under arm.

No one had ever seen Sandy try a shot himself, yet he knew every foot of the Old Course. Unlike most caddies, he had the 'grand merit' of silence during any matches in which he was involved, and it was always expected that he would put the correct club into his *man's* hand without being asked.

FEATHERIES AND INTERLOPERS

As the number of golf players increased, there arose a demand for the services of a golf professional who could coach others. In time, the good caddie became a golfer as well.

The transition from the status of senior caddie to golf professional is clearly defined in the Robertson family. David was the last of the senior caddies, while his son Allan, born on 11 September 1815, was the first professional. Allan, said to be the greatest golfer who never won an Open, succeeded in combining the duties of caddie and coach. His skill earned him many honours and recognition as the first of the truly great players, but sadly he died from an attack of jaundice at the age of 44 in 1859, the year before the first ever Open Championship. Just before Allan died, he went around the Old Course in 79, becoming the first man to break 80 on that course. His record stood for 10 years until Tom Morris bettered it.

Besides carrying clubs, mid-nineteenth-century caddies were also employed as ballmakers. Between 1840 and 1848, Allan Robertson employed two other local caddies, Tom Morris and Lang Willie, in making the feather balls known as featheries. Their workshop was Robertson's kitchen, and the balls were sold for 1/8d a ball or £1 a dozen from a window at the back of the house which overlooked the Old Course.

The featherie was the first ball made specifically for golf. Tom Morris said of it, "you were just like a shoemaker, after you filled the *lum hat* with feathers, you stuffed them into a little pocket of tough leather and began to sew." The design had definite drawbacks: a ball was seldom round, and it was prone to sogginess which led to its rapid disintegration. In spite of that, the featherie remained virtually unchanged until the gutta percha ball, or guttie, was introduced to Scotland in 1849 and found to be both cheaper and more durable.

Caddie John Fenton, circa 1890. John was said to have a grand face for funerals, and was always known as 'Treacle', indicating that there was a kind of pathos about him which lasted all the time, much like treacle (molasses) taking forever to run!

THE GUTTIE

There is some speculation as to the inventor of the first guttie ball, but the strongest claim comes from the Reverend Dr. R. Paterson of St. Andrews, who claimed that in 1845, a Hindu statue was shipped to St. Andrews from India packed with "chunks and chips" of gutta percha to prevent damage. As a young boy he discovered it was malleable and fashioned a piece into a ball. His attempts to strike it with a club showed great promise and with perseverance he discovered it flew better and was more durable than the featherie. He later emigrated to America to become a clergyman, but before going he wrote,

> I quit St. Andrews for a louder call,
> and left to golfers all I had, a ball.

As the new ball was inclined to break up in mid-flight, a rule was devised which read, "If a ball splits into separate pieces, another ball may be laid down where the largest portion lies." The guttie's introduction united the caddies in a campaign against it because they thought that part of their living was gone. Headed by Allan Robertson, who in 1844 had sold the considerable number of 2,556 featheries, they boycotted the 'new stuff,' which they said was *nae gowf.* Robertson himself actually attempted to buy up all the gutties found amongst the *whins* by the caddies and even tried to destroy the "interlopers" by fire!

All these efforts were in vain, however, and by 1848 the guttie became widely accepted. In fact, this improvement, along with the opening in 1852 of a new railway linking St. Andrews with Edinburgh and Glasgow, resulted in an enormous increase in the number of people taking up golf and requiring a caddie's service. Thus, contrary to their original fears, things could not have been better for the caddies.

Robertson finally realised he had been mistaken about the guttie, and along with Bob Kirk, another senior caddie and a fine golfer, took to the "new stuff" with such enthusiasm that caddying now took second place to their ballmaking.

There were other changes which resulted from the increased use and popularity of the Old Course. One was the widening of the links with new holes being made, one for the outward and one for the inward players, rather than the single hole on each green. The Old Course originally had 22 holes, 11 out and 11 in. The course started on the hill just behind the R&A Clubhouse with only one flag on each green, and homeward players had the right-of-way to play onto the putting surface. This layout was changed to 18 holes in 1764. At a meeting of the Society of St. Andrews Golfers, a Minute reads:

> The Captains and Gentlemen golfers are of the opinion that it would be for the improvement of the links that the first four holes should be converted into two.

Today, there are seven double greens on the Old Course, and homeward players still have the right-of-way, with the exception of hole number one, where those playing the eighteenth must give priority to the players on the first fairway setting out on their round.

The other important change had to do with the teeing up of the ball. When the guttie with its truer roll made the featherie obsolete, the rules of golf, especially those relating to the green, had to be modified. In 1777, the teeing ground was described as "not nearer than one club length, not further than four club lengths from the hole." By 1822 this had been changed to read "not nearer than two club lengths," and much later it became six club lengths from the hole. Then in 1882, the R&A rules stipulated that the diameter of the hole was to be four inches, increased in 1891 to 4-1/4 inches. The greens were now becoming a recognised well-mown surface used only for putting. The guttie had in essence brought the tee off the green, and the teeing ground as we know it came into being.

Learning from Your Elders

A young caddie watches intently as the champions of the day pose for a photographer on the St. Andrews links, circa 1855.

Auld Kirky, on the far right, has left his box for a round of carrying—the young caddie may have already been a customer of his for a 'Kirky remake'. Caddie/clubmaker James Wilson stands on the left, and bending down in the foreground is Allan Robertson. Auld Daw stands to Kirky's right. The caddie in the central background is Bob Andrew ('The Rook').

KIRKY'S REMAKES

Robertson and his crew were not the only guttie entrepreneurs in St. Andrews. Auld Kirky was a ballmaker who had also been a caddie for many years. He had a box which was situated just opposite George Leslie's Inn in Golf Place. Every day he sat there, cutting up new gutta and boiling the pieces in a little stew-pan. He would then take a piece in each hand and squeeze the material until it was ready for the mould. Once shaped, the balls were taken out, dried, and allowed to firm.

Although on the green the guttie was more consistent than the featherie, the ball was inclined to drop in flight because it was uniformly round and smooth. Eventually, players realised that after the ball became cut and hacked with usage, it flew better. After this, Auld Kirky began hammering each ball in an egg-shaped cup, using a hammer with a broad blade until the ball was more or less symmetrically nicked, then finally giving it a coat of paint. He was also known for his remakes, and the 'box' was very popular with the younger lads who had saved a sixpence for a Kirky remake.

Caddie Profile: Lang Willie

"pit yer right foot in the fifth position,
an' pay *attenshin tae* the fiddle! *"*

Willie Robertson, or 'Lang Willie' as he was known, was much taller than most of his contemporaries. Measuring 6'2", with bent knees and a slouching gate, he was unmistakable in his white moleskin *breeks*, said to be *mither-made*, and a *lum hat* which made him look like a veritable giant. Willie always swore by milk, saying that it was all he would drink, much to the amusement of Allan Robertson, who knew his true drinking habits.

Apart from his reputation as an outstanding caddie, Lang Willie enjoyed playing the fiddle, and was indispensable at weddings. He also taught the *fisher lasses* dancing, and when his services were sought out as a golf coach, he sometimes bewildered his pupils when giving advice on the proper stance: "pit yer right foot in the fifth position, an' pay attenshin *tae* the fiddle! *"*

Willie suffered several strokes whilst on the golf course. After one, a fellow caddie asked him how he had felt at the time, and Willie answered, "I felt *naething*." Later, his sister said his face looked pale and twisted in the morning. "Nonsense!" cried Willie, but later added, "When I sat *doon tae ma porritch, ma* jaw *widnae* work." He later died of a heart attack while carrying on the Old Course.

RUBBING UP

Although his knowledge of both the links and the game itself was important when a caddie was given a job, his first duty was the rubbing-up of his golfer's clubs. Indeed, during the nineteenth and early twentieth centuries, caddies were paid a tip not for carrying their golfer's clubs but for cleaning them before and at the end of the round.

The task was not taken lightly. Before a round began, the caddie would remove his *man's* clubs from the wooden box in which they had been transported and stored in the clubhouse, undoing the strap which tied the clubs together. He would then pick up the clubs in a tight bundle and carry them under his arm to the bench, where the "rubbing-up" began.

A piece of old emery paper was an essential part of the caddie's equipment because it burnished the metal but did not scratch. He first rubbed along the blade of the iron, front and back, then across at the point and heel. According to Tom Morris, this was done "so as to leave the centre with a different shade from the rest of the club that the eye might be more easily caught when aiming the ball."

The caddie also took pride in having all the woods nicely oiled, and he would put a polish on them like that "on the back of an otter," using a hare's foot lightly dipped in linseed oil from an old tin can. In this way, the shafts developed a skin which made them weather any rain. Hugh Philp's workshop was used for this duty and an old bench was given over to the caddies to 'clean up' their golfer's clubs.

EARLY CLUBMAKERS

The earliest clubmaker in St. Andrews was Hugh Philp, now recognised as the finest clubmaker ever. He had a small workshop which stood a little below the steps of the Marine Hotel (now the Rusacks) alongside the eighteenth fairway of the Old Course. Most of his employees came from the younger caddies, and those showing most interest in the game were made apprentice clubmakers.

James Wilson, who eventually became a recognised clubmaker himself, was the first caddie to work for Old Philp. He eventually took over Philp's workshop in 1852, also employing caddies, such as the legendary Andra' Strath, as apprentice clubmakers. After Hugh Philp's death in 1854, Robert Forgan took over the entire business from James Wilson. Out of the Forgan stable of caddie-cum-apprentices came the famous Jamie Anderson, who became a three-time winner of the Open Championship, winning in 1877, 1878 and 1879. Jamie was the eldest son of 'Auld Daw' Anderson, who was said to have put two of his family through university with not only the proceeds of his ginger beer sales near the ninth hole of the Old Course, but by selling a wee nip or two to the golfers who, on cold and windy days, took advantage of the 'secret stash' under his "wicker basket on wheels"! Jamie later went on to become a very fine clubmaker himself, continuing the tradition of employing caddies in his workshop. Indeed, no less than two future Open winners were to be apprenticed to him. The most colourful of these was Bob Martin, who won the Open twice but described his rather flat swing as that of "an old wife cutting hay."

Bob Martin, St. Andrews caddie and professional golfer, went on to win the Open Championship in 1876 and 1885. He was noted for his long drives and was especially gifted in his use of the cleek. Though a fine golfer, he described his swing like an "old wife cutting hay."

Caddie Profile: Auld Daw

"A wee nip just to warm the inner man!"

Caddie David Anderson, a fine golfer and later Keeper of the Green for the R&A, whose son Jamie won the Open Championship three times in succession, was one of the most respected of the senior caddies. 'Auld Daw' started carrying when still a schoolboy, was once employed by Allan Robertson as a ballmaker, and caddied for Allan throughout most of his professional life. He is better known for his ginger beer stall, which he set up at the ninth hole of the Old Course upon his retirement. He used to offer ginger beer to the thirsty golfer or better yet, a *wee nip (just to warm the inner man!!)* from the flask which he had discreetly hidden in his hip pocket.

This ginger beer bottle was found by the author during a maintenance excavation at the site of Auld Daw's original ginger beer stall near the ninth hole of the Old Course. Bottles like this were common in the late nineteenth century.

BAGPIPES AND CANVAS CONTAINERS

The number of clubs carried in those early days rarely exceeded six, so the caddie was able to carry them loosely underarm like a set of bagpipes. This practice lasted until the ever-increasing number of clubs used in the game led to the introduction of the first golf bag in 1890, the year that the 'Dr. Trails Canvas Container' made its first appearance on the Old Course.

This canvas container, or golf bag as it became known, was referred to as a *poke* by the local caddies. 'Auld Daw,' on being asked for whom he was caddying, replied, "I *dinna ken,* but he's got a *poke o' baffies* like a stag's *heid.*" Most of the professional golfers who travelled any great distances carried their clubs in wooden boxes, like mobile lockers. Although the canvas container made the job of carrying clubs easier, some senior caddies still continued to carry the clubs loose underarm, with the heads pointing downward for easy recognition. They were able to hand the club to their *man* much quicker than the 'bag toter.'

After handing the club to his *man,* an additional task of the caddie was to run forward and spot where the ball had landed. Without this type of precaution, the ball could quite easily have been lost in the heavy gorse and sandy wastes on the links. A local paper reported in 1920 that a caddie who was careless in his duties was given a *wee skelp* (light tap) *on the heid* to make him pay attention. Although painful, the writer added, it was also quite profitable, as the tap was worth sixpence to the injured caddie. Perhaps this explains the reported rise in caddie offences during this period!

Above: caddies James Miles and Alex Elder outside the caddie box, conforming to the new regulation dress code. Their caddie badges can be seen on their jacket lapels.

Right: caddie badge, circa 1899. Because of the need for regulation, caddies were required to register to work on the links, and work was only given to those who could produce their caddie badge or armband.

Caddie Profile: 'Sodger' Mcintyre

John Smith Mcintyre was a quiet man but made himself one of the personalities of the links at a time when the Caddy Shelter was already rich in characters. Sodger, as he was known, started carrying clubs when just a boy, learning all the finer points of the game. He was a good golfer, but preferred to caddie. During the latter part of his career, Sodger caddied for Prime Minister A. J. Balfour, who after a bad shot would always say to him, "If I always got what I wanted, I would never play golf."

Sodger Mcintyre was one of the last of the Old Brigade of caddies. In 1936 he was 71 years old, and he decided to retire after 60 years on the links. Reminiscing about his younger days, he could remember back to Young Tom Morris and the time when the Old Course was much narrower than it is today. "Bunkers in his day were bunkers," enthused Sodger. "Ye used *tae* climb 15 feet *doon intae* the bowels o' Hell, but Hell Bunker's *no'* like hell *ata' noo*. Today, it's a kind o' paradise in hell, with *mair* sand than brimstone, and we only had up *tae* eight clubs *tae* carry, a wooden driver, a *spoon* for second shots, a *mid-spoon*, a *baffy*, a *niblick* and yer putter. With up to twenty-five clubs in a golfer's bag today, caddies are weighed under *wi' a'* that tackle!"

Sadly, Sodger died a year after retiring, but many tributes were paid to him. Roger Wethered, for whom Sodger caddied when he won the Amateur Championship, and former Prime Minister Balfour, returned to St. Andrews to pay tribute to a "fine gentleman."

DOG CADDIES

From the turn of the century, another type of creature became popular on the Old Course amongst golfers and caddies alike. Newcomers would have been surprised to see dogs and men moving in and out of the gorse, no doubt thinking them to be poachers after rabbits. They were, in fact, the dog-caddies and dog-men of St. Andrews.

The dog-caddie, or ball finder, was a dog which was carefully trained to find golf balls. It had long been a recognised custom (continued by some merchants in the present day) that anyone finding balls could sell them to the local clubmakers or shopkeepers, and some of the men at that time could earn upwards of £1 a day with a well-trained dog. If a player lost his ball amongst the *whins* and any of the dog-men were about, they would come across to him and strike a deal. After it had been concluded, the dogs were sent into the *whins* and the player was almost certain to have his ball retrieved.

Since 1921, caddies and golfers have been restricted to looking for balls on the links during the hours from 8pm to 8am only. Some caddies have found to their cost that ignoring this regulation is a sure way of losing rather than making money. One caddie, taken to the old Burgh Police Court under the bye-law, was accused of using his dog to search for balls amongst the *whins* outside the allowed hours. When charged with this offence, the caddie maintained that he was only taking his dog for a walk on the lead. What he failed to explain was that the lead was forty yards long and didn't hinder the dog from making a wide search of the *whins!* When he was fined £1 or ten days in the local jail, he offered to pay the £1, saying that his dog would miss the exercise on the links if he weren't around!

There was also talk of a 'ball-finders' badge being given to those caddies too old to carry clubs, which would allow them to supplement their pensions and at the same time keep them out in 'God's fresh air.' More importantly, it would keep them away from the pubs and their own houses, where they were "nothing but a nuisance" to their already overworked wives!

'Wiggy' Ayton carries his golfer's clubs loose under arm.

LOCAL LORE

The time spent between jobs was a good chance for a caddie to practice his game. Because there was nowhere to practise, the caddies themselves converted a spare piece of ground near the old railway station into a caddies' course, to encourage the younger lads to learn the *game o' gowf*. The location chosen was a piece of rough ground just opposite the seventeenth hole on the Old Course, and the caddies laid out four holes known as the 'Scholars.' Part of this land is now occupied by the Old Course Hotel.

Around the same time, caddies laid out a short putting area on the site of the present Rusacks Hotel. There they would while away the hours until their services were needed or the local pubs opened, whichever came first! But some 'outsiders' disputed the caddies' exclusive rights to the green. While waiting for their husbands to finish their rounds on the Old Course, wives of R&A members would venture onto the 'Caddies Course'. While the caddies were annoyed by this intrusion, it was not in their interest to formally complain, because it was not unusual for members' wives to assist the caddies and their families in lean times by providing them with food and clothing.

The caddies tolerated this situation for many years, until the R&A decided it was in everyone's best interest to look for an exclusive site for the ladies, well away from the critical eyes of the caddies! Today, this putting green is known worldwide as the Himalayas, and has been the home of the Ladies Putting Club since 1867.

The gallery looks on intently as members of the Ladies Putting Club play an early match over the famous Himalayas putting green, before the turn of the century. Most ladies employed young caddies, since the tight corsets popular during this period did not allow the ladies to bend over to retrieve the ball from the hole!

The Ladies Putting Club remained a private club, used by R&A members and their wives, until after the Second World War, when due to financial constraints it was opened to the public. Today, presidents, professionals and the general public all enjoy their round on what is arguably the oldest and most unique putting course in the world.

THE SWILCAN BURN

Prior to the first Open Championship at St. Andrews, the Swilcan Burn was a natural sandy-edged water hazard which swept almost into the centre of the first fairway, not the well-defined narrow channel it is today. To make things even worse, the burn was used by the women of the town to wash and bleach their clothes and sheets, and the washing was then laid out on the fairway and on the surrounding *whin* bushes to dry. The R&A introduced several local rules to handle this unique domestic infringement on the game. In 1851 a new rule was introduced to the effect that, "When a ball lies on clothes, or within one club length of a washing tub, the clothes may be drawn from under the ball and the tub removed." In 1888 the rule was changed to read: "When a ball lies on clothes, the ball may be lifted and dropped behind, without penalty." Golfers must have breathed a sigh of relief when the new local public laundry was built near the East Sands, just opposite the harbour!

Major Boothby is playing to the original first green on the Old Course, circa 1880. To his right is Jamie Anderson, caddie and Open champion in 1877, 1878 and 1879, while standing on the Swilcan Bridge behind him are 'Auld Daw' Anderson and Allan Robertson. Tom Morris Senior, at the far left, looks on intently.

Even without the washing, playing the first hole was a far different experience in those days. The Swilcan Burn would have been reachable from the first tee and the fairway was less than a third of its present width, with the rest a sandy natural hazard. Granny Clark's Wynd was a dirt path leading to the beach, and was used to transport the town's lifeboat across the Old Course and onto the West Sands for launching. When Halkets bunker * was filled in and the sandy area reclaimed, the first and eighteenth fairways were left the wide bunker-less area we know today.

There were many ways of using the Swilcan Burn to earn extra money. A favourite trick was to go further up the burn and stir up the water, making it cloudy at the point where the water today crosses the first and eighteenth fairways. After this, golfers who put their balls in the burn had no chance of finding them. Later that day, the young caddies would fish out the balls from the now clear water and sell them back to the golfers for 1d, or 2d for extra good ones! It was said that when your ball fell into the Swilcan Burn, the young caddie would stamp it into the mud, and then be good enough to try and find it for you. The older caddies would studiously *howk* for stray balls amongst the *whins*. It was believed the employment in both cases was very lucrative!

In fact, the caddies' ingenuity in such matters was nearly boundless. Prior to the lining of the holes on the Old Course with tin in 1890, there were no sand boxes beside the tees. The usual ploy was for the caddie to scoop some sand from the bottom of the hole on each green and use it to tee his golfer's ball at the next hole. More enterprising caddies would carry a small bag of sand around their necks. But many of the younger caddies carried this even further: a common prank was

---

* Halkets bunker, which was filled in prior to 1873, used to lie on the town side of the first fairway of the Old Course just opposite Granny Clark's Wynd.

to deepen the hole to about 12 inches so that the golfer could not retrieve his ball!

An Important Putt

The gentleman in the black 'lum hat' is Sir Hugh Lyon Playfair, circa 1858. Sir Hugh was an inveterate golfer and was in the habit of monogramming his personal items (clubs, umbrella, etc.) with the slogan, "This was stolen from Sir Hugh Lyon Playfair" in an attempt to prevent his possessions from 'innocently going astray!'

SILLYBODKINS AND SCHOLARS

A stranger passing Allan Robertson's house on the corner of Golf Place would wonder at a dozen or so men and boys, some leaning against the wall of Allan's house gazing over the nearby Lucklaw Hill, anxious that the wind should be "*aff the nairth*" as a sign of good weather. Others, hands in pockets, would be walking up and down contemplating their chances of work that day.

If it was a doubtful morning, Allan would always send senior caddie Charlie Thomson, a self-professed authority on the weather, across to the Old Union Parlour to read what the glass said on the barometer. On his return, Charlie would always say, "I'm o' the *opeenion* that she's further *doon* the day than she was yesterday." Asked what he meant he would reply, "Well Sir, *ah'm jist dootin'* that it'll be very wet, or we'll get *mair* rain. Either way, the rain is God's way o' cleanin' the *coos!*" But even Charlie's ambiguous remark would not daunt the player bent on his round of golf.

If there was not much to do, young boys bent on self-improvement could be seen copying the swings of the senior caddies. Golf balls were too expensive for the caddies to buy, so they would improvise by using *chuckie stanes* (pebbles) or better yet corks, in endless supply due to an apparently free flow of champagne and claret, possibly increased by fines paid by the Gentlemen Golfers after transgressing the rule on payment to caddies!

Sandy Herd, a local caddie and golfer, tells of the ingenuity of the caddie. To make these claret-sodden corks carry against the wind of which St. Andrews gets its fair share, they hit on the idea of inserting screw nails into them to give the corks weight. For some reason not

explained by Sandy, they were given the name of *sillybodkins* by the
caddies. Sandy went on to become the Open winner in 1902, which
was the first time in a major British tournament that the new Haskell
ball was used, an innovation which was to change the game much more
than the introduction of the guttie.

*Sandy Herd and his caddie 'Pauchy' Aitken, circa 1903. Leading up to the 1902 Open
in Hoylake, England, Sandy Herd's game was in poor shape (described by Harold Hilton
as 'in decadence') but his last minute switch from his favourite guttie to the new Haskell
ball was to put 20-30 yards on his game. Before teeing off on his first round for the Open,
he gave the new ball scant praise. By the time he had won the Open, however, he enthused
to anyone and everyone who would listen! Sandy was always recognisable from the distance
by the number of waggles he took before striking the ball!*

RIBBED AT ST. ANDREWS

The year 1873 saw the Open Championship leave Prestwick for the first time since its inception in 1860 and come to St. Andrews. A directive was sent out to all Clubs stating that competitors must be known, honest and respectable caddies. The tournament was won by 'Young' Tom Kidd, a local caddie whose father also caddied on the links. Tom was well-known as the longest driver among the professional golfers at that time, and he also introduced the 'ribbed' club, an innovation which considerably aided his Open win. Tom had confided to his friends that he had found a way to play the slippery greens at St. Andrews and boasted, "Ye'll see me *dae* it!" He went on to justify his boast. As the other balls slithered over the greens, Tom's stood stock-still beside the hole. He had carved the face of the clubs with a file which made them as rough as a *peerie* (spinning top). The following year, 26-year-old Tom Kidd set out to defend his title and came in a close second to Tom Morris.

Photo insert of Tom Kidd from a golfing diploma produced in 1910 to commemorate the golden jubilee of the Open Championship. Note that Tom is wearing his Open Winner medal on his jacket lapel. Tom, like many professional golfers, earned a reputation as an expert teacher to many novices, instilling the importance of the 'grip and stance.'

Unfortunately, prize money for those early tournaments was very little—the big money matches were still played between professionals and club members. This was of no benefit to Tom Kidd, though, because he was a local lad who preferred working the links of St. Andrews as a caddie to travelling further afield for the higher stakes, like Tom Morris and his peers. For Tom Kidd, the Open winnings amounted to only £11 plus the medal itself, and a year to the day of winning the championship, Tom actually had to sell that medal to raise money for his forthcoming marriage. Ten years later, on the 16th of January 1884, Tom Kidd died of a heart attack at his home in Rose Lane.

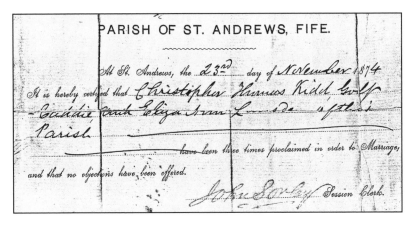

Thomas Kidd's marriage certificate, 1874.

The Links Act of 1894 meant that patronage of the R&A was reduced and responsibility for the caddies now came under the control of the Burgh Court. Special bye-laws were introduced, including the first set of rules for the licensing of caddies. These bye-laws were implemented by the Town Council in 1896.

THE TWENTIETH CENTURY

FISHERMEN AND FOREIGNERS FEES

At the start of the twentieth century, caddying as a primary occupation was considered a dead-end job, and the traditional caddie—the "old worthy"—came from the poorer people of the town. But now a different type of man began to join the ranks: the local fisherman, who turned to caddying to supplement his ever-decreasing earnings from the declining St. Andrews fishing industry. Along with this change came a change in the public's attitudes towards caddies, who were no longer considered 'ragamuffins' and were becoming more respectable, if not altogether respectful of the golfers!

The regular caddies were not against the 'foreigners,' as they were called, but tradition stated that when a new fisherman had his first caddie fee, he used it to buy drink for the regular caddies. Occasionally this was the prelude to a celebration, and some of the caddies would take to the course the worse for drink. On one occasion, one of the senior caddies called 'Old Grant' was told by his *man*, "You're drunk, I won't have a drunk caddie." Scathingly came Grant's reply: "Maybe I'm drunk, but I'll get sober, you *cannae gowf* and ye'll no' get better!" Off he staggered, scattering his *man's* clubs over the ground!

When they began caddying regularly, the fishermen added a sartorial touch to the links by wearing their fisherman's garb of blue woollen jerseys and peak caps. This sort of 'uniform' became a regular sight on the links for many years. Apart from the fishermen, men from other trades began to rely on golf to supplement their incomes, and many were provided with employment through the continued popularity of the game. Clubmaking and *cleekmaking* gave many blacksmiths work, and joiners combined clubmaking with housebuilding. Many ex-servicemen coming home from the wars took up caddying on their return to civilian life.

Caddies David Melville and John Chisholm, circa 1900. These two retired fishermen took to caddying as the local fishing trade became less lucrative. Their mode of dress brought a sartorial note to the Caddie Shelter.

Caddie Profile: Donal' Blue

Donal' caddied on the links for 'donkey's years,' as he put it. A fisherman by trade, he combined his nets and clubs when the fishing industry in St. Andrews began to decline.

Donal' and his sidekick 'Stumpie Eye' were the heroes of an annual golf match played over the Old Course with a purse of £5 for the winner, put up by the members of the R&A and visitors to the links. This was no ordinary match, for as the players made their way around the course, young lads would gather the men's divots and throw them at their heads as they attempted a shot, or use them to cover their balls. All this led to quite a bit of abuse from Donal' and Stumpie, and the end of the match usually took the form of a *dookin* with both players being thrown into the Swilcan Burn! The two friends were always followed by several hundred spectators who roared continuously at the pantomime. But despite Donal's antics, he was a very good golfer and a respected caddie.

Donal' Blue in one of his many guises, circa 1890. Donal' was the first caddie to go commercial by having postcard photographs of himself printed, which he sold to visiting golfers! He is seen here performing for tourists outside the St. Andrews Castle grounds, where, when not caddying or posing, he worked as a part-time Keeper of the Castle.

Caddie Profile: Henry J. Clarke

Sodger Mcintyre's *auld buddy* Henry J. Clarke, another of the senior caddies, died about two weeks after Sodger. Always known by his full name, Clarke lived about three miles outside St. Andrews and he would walk to the links every day, caddie, then walk the three miles home again.

Clarke joined the Royal Navy in 1880 and then joined the Highland Light Infantry, doing service in the Boer War. Later, he served with his regiment at the relief of Khartoum. After the Army, he returned to his first love, the links, but never forgot his military ways, sporting the widest 'military moustache' ever seen on the course! His pall bearers were all R&A Club members, such was the esteem in which the *auld yins,* the traditional caddies, were held.

CODES AND CLOOTS

In 1920, the R&A decided that during medal weeks, the caddie fees were to be reduced by 1/- per round, and any other matches played by members were reduced by 6d a round. The caddies, although very unhappy about the changes, had no alternative but to accept, as there was then no recourse that they could employ. The local magistrates, along with the R&A, had absolute control of the caddies, who were told that they must "accept the new charges, or no licence would be issued."

By 1928, the Town Links Committee had again revised the bye-laws relating to caddies, and had introduced a new voucher system which gave the Caddie Superintendent even more control over the caddies. Later that year, the Committee hired a new Caddie Superintendent, Mr. Fyfe, who increased the fee from the rate of 1/6d per round, which had been in effect for several decades, to 3/- for men and 1/6d for the younger boys. Using this increase as leverage, Fyfe introduced a much-needed new code of discipline.

Since the cleaning of the golfer's clubs was still considered the caddie's primary duty, Fyfe would only give work to those caddies who produced the requisite piece of emery cloth for the job, and any caddie turning up for work without his *cloot* was sent home for the day. An initial cleaning of the golfer's clubs was required before going out on the course, because Fyfe believed it made them "easier to clean after each round." Fyfe was also noted for his unique way of settling disputes between caddies. He would send them to the nearby town bandstand, out of sight of the Club and golfers, with instructions to "go to the bandstand and fight as long as you can stand, then come back and then I'll find you work!"

About this time, an article in the local newspaper mentions a fisherman/ caddie named Buff Wilson who, having completed his round, received no tip from the golfer. When the golfer asked Buff if he would turn up at 8am the next morning, Buff, looking first at his voucher and then at his golfer (who was also a fisherman), said in his most *pawky* tone, "Yer no feared to ask me to come *aff* ma boat at that time in the mornin', for *nae mair* than a voucher, three shillin', eighteen clubs, o'er seven miles o' ground, as yer in a habit o' playin'. I think I'd be better at the nets, or under the blankets sleepin'!"

During the 1930s the local Town Council instigated a campaign to rid the courses of unregistered caddies. Two caddies were arrested and brought before the Court along with the golfer who was charged with employing them. As appearances at the Court increased, so did the fines.

Caddie licence, 1924.

Tackety Boots and Cloth Bunnets

Caddies, 1924. These caddies are sitting on the bench used for 'rubbing up' the golfers' clubs. Tips were paid for the quality of this work, not necessarily the caddies' performance on the course.

In the background is the old Caddie Shelter which was built in 1891 on the site of what is now the car park by the R&A Clubhouse. The Caddie Superintendent's office is on the left of the building, and the canopy on the right was used by both caddies and the public, since the site of the shelter was "public land."

UNDER ONE ROOF

In 1891, the R&A petitioned the Town Council against the "general behaviour" of the caddies. It was claimed that caddies booked by members were not turning up on time, nor were they prepared to work for the set caddie fee. The Town Council sympathised with the caddies, especially Provost George Murray, who said, "The Club are at fault, they do not engage caddies through the Caddie Master." It was found that the Club expected caddies to be booked and then wait indefinitely for certain members who seldom turned up on time, with no 'waiting time' payable to the caddies. Since visitors were offering more money, the caddies gradually moved to these more lucrative customers. The situation led to some bad feeling between caddies and the Club, and the R&A were reminded that they must book their caddies through the Caddie Master, who was paid to look after the caddies' interest.

This incident was one of many which led the caddies that same year to petition the Town Council to have a Caddie Shelter erected near the flagpole opposite the R&A Clubhouse. The flagpole came from the sailing ship Cutty Sark, and was now the property of the R&A, which used it to fly the Club's standard. This had become a popular area for golfers and caddies to meet up prior to their rounds. The request was agreed to the following year, but as this ground was public land, the Town Council decided that the shelter could not be for the exclusive use of caddies alone, and that the public would have the right to shelter under the building's veranda.

In the early 1930s, a proposal went before the Town Council for the building of a new Caddie Shelter, since the old one was now considered too close to the R&A clubhouse. The new shelter would incorporate

"a Caddie Master's office, a urinal and washing facilities, at a cost of
£316," but the ablutions were apparently more than the budget allowed
for and it was not until the present Caddie Pavilion was built that any
consideration was given to the caddies' personal needs. The shelter
was extended in 1932, but much to the caddies' disappointment still
did not include either a lavatory or any means of lighting. This extension
was partitioned off in the late 1970s and converted to a golf shop, run
by a local golf teacher, Mr. McAndrew. From that time until the caddies
were housed in their present pavilion, the caddies and shop owner merely
tolerated each other's existence.

The present Caddie Pavilion was built in 1992 and opened in February
1993. It includes toilets, drying room, washing facilities, colour TV,
food and drinks machines—how times have changed! Thankfully, the
role of the caddie, and the caddies' welfare, is as much a consideration
as any of the other improvements made by the Links Trust.

In the Bleak Midwinter

*Caddie Pavilion under snow, 1995. Most caddies must look for alternative work during
the winter months.*

Caddie Profile: Sid Rutherford

"Chicken, sir!"

Sid Rutherford was one of two brothers, both in their late 70s, who were always vying to be first on the daily list. If his brother Willie was down at the Caddie Shelter by 5am one morning, Sid would make sure he got down the next day at 4:30am. One day during an R&A medal round, Sid and his man were on the first green with the flag just a few yards from the Swilcan Burn. Sid was motioned to stand away from the flag, and he forgot that the burn was just behind him. He took a few backward steps and in he tumbled, clubs and all, followed very quickly by his golfer, not to retrieve Sid but to save his clubs!! After draining out his golf bag, in went the golfer again, this time to collect Sid!

Sid Rutherford could always be heard on the greens with his constant plea to golfers: "Hit the ball, sir, the hole will no come to you, so it won't." If a ball came up short of the hole, Sid would exclaim that the golfer was "Kentucky fried." When asked what he meant, he would respond with a wry smile, "Chicken, sir!"

THE CADDIE'S LOT

Prior to 1938, when the R&A and USPGA jointly agreed to limit the number of clubs carried by any one player to fourteen, there was no limit on the amount of clubs a golfer could carry, and many players would take as many clubs as their bags would hold. The hapless caddie might find himself lugging anything up to 22 clubs in a bag, and indeed there were now so many clubs that their identities were reduced to numbers, not names.

For the old-time golfers such excess seemed to reduce the player's need to develop his shot-making skills, and the R&A stated that "players were virtually buying shots," with the belief that good play depended on having an absurd number of clubs in their bags. For the professional, there was a waning of the traditional feeling that each club had its own identity, hand-picked, each a valued and trusted friend. Allan Robertson, for example, had his own names for all his clubs: 'The Doctor,' 'The Frying Pan,' 'Sir Robert Peel,' etc., each with a specific task. When the 1938 rule became widely known, some of the more well-known professional golfers, including Henry Cotton, declared the new rule "entirely unnecessary… golfers should be allowed to carry as many clubs as they want." They pointed out that caddies "are well remunerated for their efforts."

One caddie not entirely in agreement was Jock Hutchinson, who had his stamina well and truly tested by one enthusiastic golfer. His *man's* leather golf bag contained twenty clubs, two dozen golf balls, a pair of golf shoes, a waterproof suit, and an umbrella. After the game, wiping the sweat from his brow and pointing to his load, he said, "Eighteen holes, six miles and *aw* this for a *twa* and six tip, it's no a caddie he wants, but a *cuddy [donkey]*!"

Another story which serves to underline the importance of paying the caddie a decent tip is the one when at the end of a round the golfer gave his caddie three pennies as a tip. The caddie laid them in his palm, saying to the player, "Sir, are ye aware that I can tell yer fortune from these three coins?" The caddie went on to volunteer that the first one told him, "Yer no' a Scotsman," to which the golfer nodded assent. "An' the second that yer no married," continued the caddie, to which the golfer nodded as well, asking about the third. "*Weel*, the third *wan* tells me that yer father *wisnae* married either!!!"

Beasts of Burden

Caddies and clubs, circa 1920. These two St. Andrews caddies are shown with a typical pre-1938 array of golf bags, most of which contain up to 20 clubs. On the right is Willie Fowls, and on the left is John 'Plum' Melville, a local clubmaker/caddie who carried for Jock Hutchison when he won the 1920 Open Championship.

Caddie Profile: Andra' Kirkaldy

"Caddying in early life, professional golf later, bring a man
into good company."

One of the last of the traditional caddies, Andra' Kirkaldy turned professional golfer and later became Honorary Professional to the R&A. Said to be the greatest golfer who never won an Open, he was notorious for his profanity on the course. When being interviewed by a local reporter on the proposal that swearing should be penalised on the golf course, Andra' said, "Quite right, the damned thing should be stamped *oot!*"

Andra' used to reminisce about his early years as a caddie, and maintained that no school board could prevent the younger lads from skipping class and wandering down to the links in the hope of getting a bag. "In those days," said Andra', "young lads born into poverty, with no way of escaping, may have thought of the old caddie adage: 'caddying in early life, professional golf later, bring a man into good company.'" Below are the last six lines of a poem by Andrew Bennet in Andra's honour:

> If ye happen tae speak
> Tae a lad wi' a cleek,
> Or a lass wi' a club, or a caddie,
> They'll be donnart and raw,
> And nae golfers ata',
> If they've no' heard o' Andra' Kirkaldy.[*]

[*] If you happen to speak to a lad with a cleek, or a lass with a club, or a caddie, they'll be stupid and raw and no golfers at all if they've not heard of Andrew Kirkaldy!

Andra' Kirkaldy as Honorary Professional to the Royal & Ancient Golf Club, tending a pin during an Autumn Medal meeting, 1920.

THE WAR YEARS

With the war in Europe, all major competitions were suspended, and there was little or no golf played until the end of the conflict in 1945. The links had a strange quiet feel about them. For those caddies not involved in the war, a caddie tournament was introduced, but never became popular, with only five caddies taking part in 1943. The links were 'no-go' areas, and the beach at St. Andrews had tank traps and gun emplacements all the way along the dunes.

During this period the Town Council gave permission to some local farmers to graze up to 150 sheep on the links from the first of April to the first of December. This number must have been exceeded at some stage, as an angry writer in the Letters column of the local newspaper wanted to know why there were "more sheep on the Old Course than blades o' grass!"

During the war years, clothing was rationed and only obtainable with coupons. One elderly R&A member who had exhumed some old clothes from his deepest wardrobe wore them for his walks by the links. One day, in the vicinity of the Caddie Shelter, he was approached by some golfers and asked if he was available to caddie and if he had any golf balls for sale. Apparently his pride was hurt at being mistaken for a caddie, and this prompted him to write a letter to the local newspaper which indignantly ended "and to cap it all to be mistaken for a St. Andrews caddie" and was signed "Ballfinder"!

Sunday golf was introduced to the Eden Course in 1941, but caddies were not allowed to work on that day until it became obvious that with the increased number of golfers playing, caddies were very much needed. Only those registered were allowed to work, with the Eden starter acting as Caddie Manager. It was also decided that caddies working on Sundays were to be paid a double fee, and any caddie not working on that day could play cheap golf on the Eden instead. A Sunday round would only cost 2/-, but not many caddies took up this offer, as they would rather be on the golf course earning "double money."

In the latter half of 1945, the Town Council agreed to increase the caddie fees, which had been decreased in 1938 and were considered to be inadequate for the work. Additional bye-laws were introduced to enable the local magistrates to adjust, when necessary, the fee paid to caddies. The present fees were 3/- for men, and 2/- for younger boys. The fees were now set at 4/- for men and 2/6d for the lads, with an annual review to be written into the bye-laws.

Before the war, 60 caddies had been licensed to work on the links, but during 1946, only 28 men applied for registration. This was one reason for reviewing the caddie fee; another was to consider lowering the age for the younger lads to 13.

When peace returned to the links, the old tradition of "playing in" the Captain of the R&A Golf Club was reintroduced. Not since 1938 had the Captain Elect played himself into office. The R&A decided not to give the traditional sovereign to the caddie who returned the Captain's ball, but there was such an uproar from the caddies and others, it was decided that the ceremony would retain all its "dignified" tradition.

Caddie Profile: 'Guy' Gillespie

"To have Guy on my side is worth a few strokes to me every time."

Wallace Boyd Gillespie, known as 'Guy,' was trained in the hotel industry, but although he was a skilled waiter he preferred the links to the kitchen, and it was as a caddie that he gained fame. Guy spent every spare moment on the links, and although he was a fair golfer, it was his keen perception of the game, and especially his knowledge of the Old Course, that built up his reputation as a caddie.

After Peter Thomson won the 1955 Open Championship at St. Andrews with Guy Gillespie as his caddie, he said of him, "I'm not sure if he belongs to me, or I to him, but he would carry for no other player when I was around, and for my part, to have Guy on my side is worth a few strokes to me every time."

Gary Player and Guy Gillespie on the Swilcan Bridge, circa 1960.

THE CADDIE TOURNAMENTS

The first tournament for caddies was held in 1819, and included in the list of competitors were the ball- and clubmakers who were caddies when not at their workbenches. It was not until 1842, however, that the first winner of the "Caddies Competition," as it had by that time become known, was officially recognised. R&A Minutes show that the Club contributed £50 in prize money, playfully referred to as "in-putts". Tom Morris, then only 21, was the first winner, with a round of 92; his father came a close second. In the same Minutes, mention is made of Allan Robertson, age 27, who was prohibited from competing since his game was considered "far superior to all others." It was believed that no-one else would have a chance if Allan played!

Throughout the years since then, there have been many caddie competitions, most organised by the caddies themselves, but none of them lasting for any significant length of time. Each event typically ended in uproar or severe bouts of drinking, considered par for the course!

For those caddies not overseas during the war years, a Caddie Tournament was organised by the Town Council and the R&A in 1939. Unfortunately, it was raining hard on the opening day and some parts of the links were flooded. As a consequence, only five caddies completed their round, with 'Bunny' Hutchinson the eventual winner, returning a score of 87. In the first year, the first prize was monetary, equal to that offered to the winner of the Open.

In the second year, the prizes were in the form of goods donated by local shopkeepers. Andra' Kirkaldy and his brother Hugh made the final, and Hugh needed a five at the last hole to win. He deliberately took seven, saying as he left the green, "Andra' can *hae* the turkey, the bottle o' whisky is *mair* in my line!" Money prizes were again introduced in the third year but the caddies were becoming greedy, and the amount of prize money on offer led to a considerable amount of cheating. The tournament was cancelled after that, to be reintroduced in 1943 with a non-monetary prize.

It was not until 1993 that an actual caddie-organised annual tournament was begun. For the first time, the tournament was played 'away from home' with a different course chosen each year. Prizes for the competition are donated by local St. Andrews merchants and hoteliers, and the more liquid ones are those most keenly played for!

Inaugural Caddies vs. Links Trust Staff Annual Golf Match, 1993. In the same year that the caddies' own tournament was begun, this Caddies vs. Staff Match started, representing a successful attempt at caddie/management liaison. The match is played over the newest of the five 18-hole courses at St. Andrews, the Strathtyrum Course, and played in October, when the players have the local 'haar' and frost to contend with. The first match was halved by a very benevolent caddie intentionally missing an easy 18" putt on the last hole for what would have been a caddie win! The caddies themselves put into practice a significant link in promoting an easier working relationship all around.

The Lure of the Links

Caddies Jim Moore, John Bradley and Alex Bain, 1996. Jim is a keen golf historian and collector of golf memorabilia. John is a former Caddie Manager, and Alex is employed by the St. Andrews University Information Technology Department during the winter months. In spite of these diverse interests, the lure of the links brings these men back each season.

MECHANICAL CADDIES

By the spring of 1950, the demand for the services of the caddie was decidedly less than before the war. One very obvious reason for this decline was the introduction of the first caddy cart to the Old Course. Late in 1949 at the R&A Autumn Medal, Lord Brabazon had introduced his "mechanical caddie" or golf trolley, a "cheap, reliable and uncomplaining substitute for a caddie." This caused great consternation amongst the caddies, who quite rightly saw it as a threat to their livelihood.

R&A Captain Lord Brabazon of Tara playing in 1952.

Lord Brabazon rewards local caddie David Deas with the traditional sovereign for retrieving his ball. Lord Brabazon's cart was instrumental in reducing the number of caddies able to work on the links.

These *barras*, as they were known by the caddies, were hired from local golf shops, but most of these local contraptions were homemade, using old pram wheels which were very narrow and inclined to spoil the greens. One R&A member, Mr. Sandy Rutherford, patented a broad-wheeled cart and introduced it to St. Andrews, and by 1956, the narrow-wheeled *barras* were banned from the Old Course.

The introduction of the trolley did for some time reduce the demand for caddies, and in 1955 the Town Council paid off the Caddie Master as unnecessary, handing over this responsibility to the Old Course starter. It was not until the early 1970s, when even the broad-wheeled caddy carts were blamed for damaging the turf on the Old Course and were withdrawn as well, that demand for caddies increased sufficiently for the position of Caddie Manager to be reinstated. Caddy carts were not reintroduced on the Old Course until 1989, and then only for a limited part of the day. In 1974, with the abolition of the Town Council after a reorganisation of local government, the St. Andrews Links Trust was established by an Act of Parliament to maintain the links and ensure continuity in the operation of the golf courses.

Caddie Manager Rick Caffrey (leftmost) and some of the caddies, 1983. They are standing outside of the old Caddie Shelter which was located behind the eighteenth green of the Old Course. The building now houses a shop selling St. Andrews Links Trust merchandise.

The increasing popularity and earnings potential of the game in general led to an improved status for the St. Andrews caddies. In 1984 they felt strong enough as a group to support each other by staging a series of one-day strikes, the first major incident since 1870. The first change the caddies demanded of the Links Trust was the introduction of a grading system which would recognise the more senior caddies. This was agreed to, with either Gold or Silver grading for caddies and Bronze for the younger junior caddies or bag carriers. On the strength of this initial success, the caddies now asked for an increase in their rates. This also was agreed upon, with new rates set at £17, £13, and £9 respectively.

But in consequence, the traditional 'double bagging' was withdrawn by the Links Trust, which considered it one of the contributing factors in holding up play, especially over the Old Course. The caddies continued their one-day strikes in the hope that the double bags would be reinstated, but it soon became clear that the Links Trust was intractable on this point and furthermore would not consider the caddies' threats to involve visiting golfers by asking them to boycott St. Andrews. Slowly and one-by-one, the caddies came back to work, with the promise that the R&A Greens Committee would in the future listen to any legitimate complaint from the caddies.

A few years later the new grading system became a source of discontent amongst the caddies, because golfers were requesting the lower-rate Silver Grade caddie at the expense of the senior caddies. It was agreed to dispense with the three-tier grading and have only Caddies and Bag Carriers, with upgrading and downgrading at the discretion of the Caddie Manager.

Caddie Billy Gunn on the Swilcan Bridge, 1997. Billy Gunn was a soldier and latterly a policeman by profession prior to becoming a caddie in 1984. In 1990, Bill took a year off from caddying locally to work the European Tour, but came off the tour at the end of the season because he would rather spend the time under "God's good air" in St. Andrews. Bill considers carrying on the links "more like a holiday every day rather than work!" For three years straight, he worked the most rounds of any caddie.

During a Dunhill Pro-Am Tournament in the mid-1990s, Bill's golfer suffered a heart attack. The professional in the match, Ronan Rafferty, immediately ran for help while Bill gave mouth-to-mouth resuscitation to the stricken player. It must have been a combination of Bill's First Aid experience and the 'wee nip' he had before the round which brought the player around briefly! Billy said, "The spirit of the links seemed to work!"

Caddie Profile: 'Tip' Anderson

"Everywhere that Tony went, Tip was sure to know."

Born and bred in St. Andrews with golf in his blood (his father was a caddie before him), Tip did not take up the game until he was 15, but he soon became a single-handicapped player. He later apprenticed as a clubmaker, but this was interrupted with National Service. Upon demobilisation, Tip went back to his trade for two years before becoming involved in caddying. It soon became obvious to him that he could earn more money from carrying than from any 'real job,' so he became a full-time caddie from 1956. Tip's big break came in 1960 when he carried for Arnold Palmer in the Open. This partnership lasted an amazing 35 years longer than any other caddie/golfer relationship. In this time, Tip shared in many of Arnold Palmer's successes, including two Open titles.

When Palmer could not make it to Scotland for the 1964 Open in St. Andrews, he recommended Tip to his friend Tony Lema. Lema had never seen the Old Course, and had only two practice rounds. But in spite of this, he went on to win the Open Championship with Tip, and after his win, he singled out Tip as the reason he had won.

WOMEN CADDIES

Until very recently, caddying in Scotland, like the game of golf itself, was staunchly chauvinistic, with only men and boys employed as caddies. Although women have never accounted for more than a small minority in the caddie ranks anywhere, English Club records mention female caddies from 1890 onwards, and women have worked in this profession for years in other parts of the world. A single nineteenth-century reference to 'girl caddies' in Scotland dates back to 1870, when girls were hired as caddies during a caddie strike at Gullane which lasted some five weeks. When things returned to normal, however, the girls were let go, and it was another seventy-odd years before they resurfaced, this time on the links at North Berwick.

During the early 1970s, a few women were taken on at St. Andrews as bag carriers, a form of junior caddie. But this half-hearted recruitment effort proved to be unsuccessful, and most of the women stayed for only a few months. Not until 1993 was there a serious attempt to attract females to the St. Andrews caddie ranks, and in that year, the first female registered bag carrier appeared on the list. After 15 months as that bag carrier, Meroë Wilson was upgraded to a caddie.

Today there are even more females working at St. Andrews, but in general, recruitment has been hampered by the standard stereotype of the caddie as drunken, foul-mouthed and unkempt. Times have changed, though, with the local image upgraded by the building of a modern Caddie Pavilion and the issue of standard waterproof wear for all registered caddies and some senior bag carriers. The local professional status has benefited by the introduction of the

Caddie Liaison Committee, which was set up to give the caddies a voice in disciplinary and procedural matters. Today, the St. Andrews caddie understands the value of image, and is as keen as his or her professional tour counterpart to develop professional standing. Meroë epitomises this positive image which must surely be a goal for any caddie hoping to work at the Home of Golf.

There are still too few women who want to be caddies but the female profile is coming to the fore and interest from them has increased. Women are fully integrated into the St. Andrews caddie system, and have proven their worth.

Above: Bag carrier armband, 1970-1985.

Left: The introduction of a Bag Carriers' Training Programme in 1997 for those wishing to eventually become caddies was highly successful. Over 50 young boys and girls completed the training, which included on-course etiquette, understanding golf rules, making up personal course yardage books, and some of the more practical aspects on how to rake bunkers, replace divots, stand by the flag, etc.

Caddie Profile: Meroë Wilson

"Golf *is* life, after all…"

"I would never have dreamed after my first round as a bag carrier in June 1993 that just over two years later I would be caddying on the Old Course in the practice rounds of the 1995 Open, nor that I should participate in games that involved some of the big names in professional golf!

When I started as a bag carrier I did not yet play golf, although my father had urged me for years to take up the game. I enjoyed the outdoor work, meeting people from all over the world and being in a male-dominated environment. I had known many of the caddies for years and they accepted me for *who* I was rather than *what* I was. I listened and learned from them: lines off the tee, yardages from various landmarks, the general rub of the greens, and I marvelled at their abilities. I can still remember the thrill of walking up the eighteenth fairway carrying a bag—there's no feeling quite like it.

The caddie manager encouraged me from the very beginning and urged me to get out, pace the courses, and make up my own books, but I didn't feel confident enough to be 'made-up' to caddie status until July 1994 when I realised I'd spent an entire week being treated and used as a caddie by the golfers I was with. I reckoned it was time to take the offered promotion! Around that same time the golf bug gripped me so I took to playing the game myself, and within a year of getting my handicap I was competing in my Club's Bronze Championship final! Although I had found I didn't need to be a player to be able to caddie, it has helped enormously with my understanding of what I am doing and I feel the golfer is more comfortable in the knowledge that I play the game myself.

I have experienced mixed reactions from golfers when I introduce myself as their caddie, but on the whole I get the feeling that it really doesn't matter as long as you can do the job. There are days when I wonder why I do it: when there's a force 9 gale blowing left to right, when the bag weighs a ton, when the golfer is having a bad day—you can't do anything right then. But all it takes is a single comment like, "she knows your game, great read, good call," to restore faith in yourself. Personally, I can't imagine *not* being a caddie. Golf *is* life, after all…"

Caddies' Nicknames

Most caddies have had nicknames, sometimes reflecting a personal characteristic or trait, and other times to hide the caddie's true identity for reasons best known only to himself!! Some of these nicknames have survived to this day either in local legend or by being handed down in the family from one generation to the other, even when their meanings have long been lost. These humorous and often affectionate names represent a tradition amongst caddies as old as the game itself, and each one has added to the richness and colour of the game.

CADDIES OF YESTERYEAR
'THE WINE OF THE COUNTRY'

The Barrel Dancer: Willie Martin was a bill-poster by trade but preferred caddying on the links.

Pawky Dave: David Corstorphine was known for his dry wit, and Andra' Kirkaldy said that nobody could better him at teeing a ball, according to the weather and the shot required.

Boosy Chas: More often than not, Charlie was to be found at the 19th hole rather than at one of the other eighteen!

Poot Chisholm: Poot was a fisherman and a somewhat disreputably-dressed caddie. When his photograph was taken one day, he looked at it and asked repeatedly whether it was really of himself. On being reassured that it was, Poot gravely said, "It's such a *humblin' sicht*."

Mathy Gorum: When sober, Mathy Gorum took to caddying, but his name was often used at temperance meetings as "the awful example!" During the winter months, Mathy tried selling razors, singing songs, or *reading heids* to make some money. In his youth, no one could equal him for steadiness of eye, and it was said that he could drive a ball from the top of a bottle. In his later years, the young caddies would get him to attempt this celebrated feat, and much to the amusement of the lads, every bottle put in front of him would be smashed in his effort!

Farnie: College taught, Farnie would fluently discuss most subjects at length, and never failed to remind the other caddies of his six years of studies.

Stumpie Eye: Archie Stump, another of the very colourful caddies, was half-blind. When he took on a job he would say, "I can carry clubs *a'* day sir, but ye'll *hae tae* watch the ball for *yersel*."

Hole-in-'is-pocket: This caddie claimed never to have lost a ball, but he got his name because when a player for whom he was carrying lost his ball, he would drop one down his trouser leg and declare, "Here it is, sir, an' no such a bad lie *efter a'*." Actually, this could prove to be expensive, and was only used when there was some money involved between the players!

Plum Melville: John Melville was a local clubmaker and caddie to Jock Hutchinson when Hutchinson won the 1921 Open Championship.

John 'Treacle' Fenton: Treacle was a fisherman said to have a grand face for funerals.

Tee-Ta-Toe: This caddie was a son of fishwife 'Teenie Bell'. When a small boy he was sent to the bakers for 'three half loafs,' and it came out as Tee-Ta-Toe. The name stayed with him all his life.

Bad Lugs: This caddie was a German who, during the First World War, was accused of being a spy. He was later executed in London.

Lang Willie: Caddie Willie Robertson stood 6'2" and always wore *lum hats* and *lang breeks* which were said to be *mither-made*.

Wiggie Ayton: Wiggie later turned professional, and since he was bald as a *coot*, was never seen on the golf course without his wig.

'Skipper' Stuart Fenton: Skipper was a fisherman noted for his big mouth and little nose: make of this what you will!

Trap Door: This caddie had an ingenious system of collecting 'lost' golf balls. He had a hollow sole in the heel of his boots with a metal plate which when opened would trap any of his golfer's lost balls.

Former American President George Bush with his St. Andrews caddie Alan Jones, before teeing off to play a round on the Old Course, 1995. This was Mr. Bush's first time in St. Andrews, and he was "thrilled and proud to play at the Home of Golf." When Alan was later asked what he thought of Mr. Bush's game, he replied, "He's no slouch at the game, although playing off a 20 handicap, he returned a net 73."

THE SPIRIT OF THE LINKS:
THE MODERN CADDIE

The Bald Eagle: No one could ever remember Jimmy Beard with any hair.

Jimmy-by-the-way: This caddie always introduced himself as "I'm Jimmy, by the way."

Pete-the-feet: Pete took size 13 in a shoe—whenever he wore them, that is!

Wallop-the-hammer: George Reid, a blacksmith by trade, caddied for Open winner James Braid.

'Paddy' Gallagher: This Irish caddie added a touch of culture to the links by having studied at medical school, and he was always civil to his *man*.

A-la-carte: This was waiter Sid McDonald, of no known address. Sid always slept rough, preferring the bunkers to a bed.

Do-nut: Alex Spence was Sid's buddy and a fellow waiter.

Evil-brew: Caddie Eddie Garland later became known as 'Kick-start' due to a kicking motion made when he got into his stride. When younger, he did time on the stage as a comedian, and he always had a story to tell with his finely-honed wit.

'Ginger' Johnstone: This caddie became Caddie Master during the R&A medal competitions and at most Open tournaments.

Others who are *working the tools* today are Tweedie, Spec's, Putt-Putt, Loppy, Telf, Crocodile, and Balty, to name only a few.

CADDIE CHRONOLOGY

1763   Old Course changed from 22 holes to the present 18.

1771   First mention of St. Andrews caddies: caddie fees set by the Society of St. Andrews Golfers.

1819   Tournament for ballmakers, clubmakers and caddies.

1822   Position of Keeper of the Green given to caddie Geordie Robertson, who was dismissed as incorrigible sometime later after severe *wiggings*.

1823   Caddie David Pirie takes over as Keeper of the Green. First playing-in of R&A Captain-Elect.

1833   Mention of highly-respected David Robertson, earliest recorded St. Andrews caddie/golfer, in George Carnegie's famous poem *Golfiana*. Upon his death in 1836, he was eulogised by Carnegie in another poem.

1840   'Auld' Daw Anderson, senior caddie, takes on the job of Keeper of the Green.

1842   Old Tom Morris, age 21, is the first recognised winner of the Caddie Competition. Allan Robertson, age 27, is prohibited from competing, as his game is considered "superior to all others."

Caddie armband, 1970-1985.

1845   Allan Robertson employs caddies Tom Morris and Lang
            Willie as feather ballmakers.

1848   Guttie ball played over the links at St. Andrews, much
            to the immediate displeasure of Allan Robertson and
            the caddies.

1850   Watty Alexander and Alex Herd take over as joint
            keepers of the Green on Daw Anderson's retirement.
            With one barrow, two shovels and a combined wage of
            £6 a year, they did a good job under the circumstances!

1852   James Wilson, first St. Andrews caddie to work for
            famous clubmaker Hugh Philp.

1856   'Auld Daw' Anderson retires as Keeper of the Green to
            set up a ginger beer stall on the ninth green of the Old
            Course.

1859   Allan Robertson, son of David Robertson and a local
            caddie who was considered the greatest golfer, goes

round the Old Course in 79, becoming the first golfer to break 80. Allan Robertson dies aged 44.

1860 First real attempt to introduce regulations for the employment of caddies.

1864 First official set of Rules and Regulations for caddies is introduced.

1865 Tom Morris appointed Honorary Professional to the Royal & Ancient Golf Club.

1870 Further Rules and Regulations for caddies proposed by the R&A. Caddies strike for higher wages.

1873 Local caddie Tom Kidd wins first Open Championship to be played over the Old Course.

1875 R&A member General Moncrieffe introduces evening classes for the younger caddies at the local Fishers School. Tom Morris is appointed Caddie Superintendent and Keeper of the Green. A revised set of Rules and Regulations are introduced.

1876 First of caddie Bob Martin's two St. Andrews Open wins, the second in 1885.

1877 First of three Open wins for local caddie Jamie Anderson (others in 1878 and 1879).

1883   R&A gives a yearly subscription of £50 plus day-old
            newspapers to a local workingmen's coffee house by the
            harbour, for caddies' use.

Caddie Stephen Martin takes time out on the Old Course, 1997.

1890   Dr. Trail's "Canvas Container" makes its first appearance
            on the Old Course. New set of Rules and Regulations
            for the employment of caddies. Caddie Benefit Fund
            set up by R&A Golf Club.

1891   First Caddie Shelter built, for use in wet or snowy
            weather. Vigilance Committee set up by caddies, headed
            by Tom Morris, to maintain order and discipline within
            the caddie ranks. Andra' Kirkaldy comes off the Caddie
            Register to become a 'professional golfer.'

1892   Twenty-one caddies receive assistance from the newly-
            established Caddie Benefit Fund.

1894   Caddie Library set up within the new Shelter.
            Patronage of caddies by the R&A reduced, and

discipline of caddies now under the control of the Burgh Court.

1896   Rules for Caddies, Fees and Registration Conditions published in local newspaper. Caddie Benefit Fund is stopped, because caddies have become increasingly unwilling to contribute to the Fund. Special bye-laws for caddies are introduced and implemented by the Town Council and the local Sheriff.

1912   Nicholas Robb's title now becomes Caddie Master.

1920   Caddie fees reduced by 1/- during R&A medal week. Dog licence (Caddie Voucher) worth 7/6d given to registered caddies to help with groceries between December and January when there was little or no work on the links.

1921   Jock Hutchinson, ex-St. Andrews caddie, emigrated to USA. He returned home to win the Open, with local caddie 'Plum' Melville caddying for him.

CADDIES

Only those persons licensed by the Links Management Committee may be employed as Caddies. They shall be engaged only through the Caddie Master.
Charges **CADDIES** per round **£8·00**
BAG CARRIERS per round **£4·00**
Note:- A gratuity may be added at the Golfer's discretion. Any infringement or misbehaviour to be reported to the Caddie Master.

Caddie Fee Board, circa 1980.

1929   Caddie Superintendent Mr. Fyfe introduces a new code
            of dress and discipline to the Caddie Shelter.

1930   Second Caddie Shelter is built at a cost of £316, sited
            behind the eighteenth green on the Old Course.

1932   Unregistered caddies taken to court and heavily fined
            for working on the links.

1934   Andra' Kirkaldy, caddie/golfer and Honorary Professional
            to the R&A Golf Club, dies.

1938   New rule introduced by the R&A and USPGA limiting
            the number of clubs carried by any one golfer to 14.
            Caddie fees reduced. Annual dinner for caddies given
            by R&A member Mr. Blackwell.

1939   Caddie tournament for those caddies not involved in
            the war, continuing for three years.

1940   Reintroduction of the Caddie Benefit Fund.

1941   Caddies paid 'double fee' for working over the Eden
            Golf Course on Sundays. Caddies also offered cheap
            golf at 2/- a round.

1945   Caddie fees increased from 3/- to 4/-. Reinstatement
            of R&A Captain playing himself into office (suspended
            during the war years). Traditional sovereign given to
            the caddie who returned the Captain's ball.

1947   Return of the Caddies' Dinner, this time hosted by Mr. Blackwell's son.

1948   Caddie Benefit Fund stopped.

1949   Lord Brabazon's cart (trolley) introduced for the first time on the Old Course.

1950   Services of Caddie Master dispensed with as "unnecessary," with caddie demand on the decline. The Old Course starter took over his duties.

1955   Guy Gillespie, local caddie, wins the Open with Peter Thomson.

1956   Trolleys banned from Old Course.

1960   'Tip' Anderson, well-known local caddie, begins longest golfer-caddie association in golf: to date, 36 years.

1964   'Tip' Anderson helps American Tony Lema win the Open.

1974   Links Trust takes over administration of caddies.

Waiting for work in the Caddie Pavilion, 1996.

1984   Series of one-day strikes for higher wages, and introduction of gold, silver and bronze grading system for caddies.

1985   Traditional "double bagging" for caddies discontinued.

1989   Trolleys reintroduced on Old Course, but only after mid-day.

1992   Caddie Liaison Committee set up to represent caddie views.

1993   Author Rick Mackenzie takes over as Caddie Manager. Inaugural Links Staff vs. Caddies golf match, now played annually over the Strathtyrum Course. Revised dress code, all registered caddies given a set of waterproofs by the St. Andrews Links Trust. First female caddie registered. Old grading system abandoned, caddies and bag carriers are now the two accepted grades.

1994   New Caddie Pavilion opens, containing modern conveniences plus the Caddie Manager's office. Caddie Rules and Advice booklet published and issued to all registered caddies.

1997   Introduction of Bag Carriers (Junior Caddies) Training Programme. Bag Carriers Rules and Advice booklet published, training certificates given to all successful bag carriers

Richard Mackenzie and Rick Gibson teamed up to win the 1994 Dunhill Cup, beating the USA 2 to 1. Mackenzie has caddied for the Canadians since the Dunhill's inception.

Caddie Bruce Sorley, 1997. Bruce is one of the more experienced caddies at St. Andrews. He started caddying in 1974 and that same year, he worked the Open with Ron Caruddo and latterly Tiger Woods in 1995, and Joost Stienhammer at the Open over Royal Troon in 1997.

Bruce has also worked the European Tour, and for many years specialised in the British Amateur events where he first met Jay Siegal in 1979, and took him through the 1980 and 1984 Opens. Bruce exemplifies the bridge that a local caddie can make into the top professional ranks, but more than anything, he enjoys working the links at St. Andrews.

LINKS CADDIE MANAGERS

CADDIE MANAGERS AND CLUB OFFICERS KNOWN AT ST. ANDREWS

Tom Morris was the first Caddie Superintendent appointed by the R&A Golf Club (in 1875) to oversee the discipline of the St. Andrews caddies. Over the years there have been many who followed in his illustrious footsteps. Unfortunately, not all have been recorded, but below is a list of those names known to date.

Tom Morris	1875
John McGregor	1890
Nicholas Robb	1891
Alexander 'Wingy' Taylor	1901
James Jolly	1910
David Corstorphine	1920
Alex Fyfe	1926
George 'Grumpy' Grant	1929
William Radley	1935 – 1940
Ted Bodle	1941

Caddie Manager Alexander 'Wingy' Taylor at St. Andrews, 1901.

From 1950, with the introduction of Caddy Carts, there was a reduction in the use of caddies. The Caddie Manager's services were dispensed with from 1950 until 1973, when the carts were banned from use on the Old Course.

CADDIE MANAGERS WHO HAVE WORKED ON THE LINKS SINCE THE LINKS TRUST TOOK OVER IN 1974

David Christie	1974 – 1975
Joseph 'Bill' Winscale	1976 – 1977
Angus Lang	1977 – 1982
Rick Caffrey	1983 – 1984
Jim Moody	1985 – 1986
Jack Semple	1987 – 1990
John Bradley	1991 – 1992
Richard Mackenzie	1993 – present

Today's St. Andrews caddies in uniform, with author Rick Mackenzie in centre.

Scottish Glossary

Ah'm jist dootin' (page 74): I'm just doubting. Caddie Charlie Thompson was hedging his bets with this remark—he'd be right either way!

aff the nairth (page 74): off the north. On a links course such as St. Andrews the wind is always a major consideration. Even if it weren't, talking about the weather is a major part of any Scotsman's day!

ata' noo (page 66): at all now. Sodger remembers when Hell bunker was deeper than it is today. In those days there was a step which took the hapless golfer into the bowels of Hell!

auld (pages 2, 14, et al.): old; in family relationships, indicating the oldest. In the golfing sense, the prefix *auld* is a mark of respect for an old man's contribution to the game.

auld buddy (page 83): a long-standing companion, who has shared many an agonizing round on the links and afterwards many a *wee nip at the 19th hole!*

awthing (page 8): anything.

baffy (baffies) (page 64): a hickory-shafted fairway wood equivalent to a modern 4 wood.

barras (page 101): barrows.

braw (page 5): brave, fine, splendid.

breeks (or **troosers**) (pages 39, 58): trousers.

bunker (page 5, et al.): similar to sand traps in the USA. Originally dug out by sheep sheltering from the cold north winds, they became one of the accepted hazards in a round of golf.

bunnet (pages 9, 41, 86): a soft, flat, brimless cap worn by men and boys, latterly usually one with a peak. These were an accepted part of the caddies' garb.

cannae gowf (page 78): cannot play golf.

cauld (page 1): cold

chuckie stanes (page 74): pebbles (or occasionally, marbles).

cleek, cleekmaking (pages 61, 79): a golf club (nineteenth and early twentieth century) corresponding to the number 4 iron.

cloot (page 84): a piece of cloth or a rag.

coos (page 74): cows.

coot (page 112): pigeon.

cuddy (page 90): a donkey or horse.

dae (pages 37, 39, 76): do

deaved (page 21): deafened; annoyed with noise or talk.

dinna (page 8): don't.

donnart (page 92): dull, stupid.

Doo Dah verses (page 40): a stylised form of mouth music without words, often practised when a man was the worse for drink but still wanted to entertain anyone who would listen, including himself! This distinctive style of music-making stopped in the middle of this century.

dookin (page 80): a drenching, a soaking.

doon (pages 39, 58, 74): down.

fu' o' ale (page 40): full of ale, drunk and legless as the case may be!

game o' gowf (page 69): game of golf.

gey cauld (page 4): very cold.
gey strang (page 1): very strong.

ghillie (page 34): a sportsman's attendant, usually in deerstalking or angling in the Highlands.

grasshoppin', workin' the land (pages 2, 3): both refer to carrying the golfer's clubs around the links.

haar (page 99): a cold mist or fog, especially a sea-fog coming off the North Sea onto the eastern coastal areas in Scotland. There is an old Scottish pun to the effect that "the *haar* is never mist!"

hae (page 99): have.

heid (pages 8, 64): head

howk (page 72): dig; figuratively: unearth, bring out, extricate.

intae (page 66): into.

ken (page 39): know.

lasses (page 58): young girls.

lang (pages 3, 5, 58, 112): long.

luggin' (pages 8, 90): carrying something.

lum hat (pages 52, 73): a tall silk hat, a top-hat. The word *lum* means a chimney, the smoke-vent or flue of a fireplace, or a chimney-stack. An old Scottish saying runs, "Lang may your lum reek, and lang may you have the wood to fire it," wishing you health and happiness.

mair (pages 66, 74): more.

man (pages 8, 9, 10, et al.): caddies' term for the golfer.

mid-spoon (page 66): see *spoon*

mither-made (pages 58, 112): mother-made. Lang Willie's mother saved money by sewing his clothes at home.

nae (pages 37, 92, et al.): no, not any.

nae mair (page 85): no more.

nae gowf (page 54): not golf.

niblick (pages 5, 66): the golf club corresponding to the number 8 or 9 iron (late nineteenth, early twentieth century). American golfer Bernard Darwin says that, "When you land in any of the pot bunkers at St. Andrews, there's only enough room for an angry man and his *niblick*!"

och (page 44): a term used to express weariness and exasperation, as in, "*Och*, man, ye cannae gowf, and yer nae likely tae!"

oor (pages 2, 8): our.

oot (pages 4, 92): out.

pawky (pages 2, 5, 85): having a matter-of-fact, humorously critical outlook on life, characterised by a sly, quiet wit.

peerie (page 76): a spinning top.

poke (page 64): a bag or pouch, a small sack; a shopkeeper's paper bag. Used by caddies to mean a golf bag.

porritch (pages 44, 58): porridge, the dish of oatmeal (or rolled oats) boiled in salted water. One of its significant properties is that it does keep you regular!

Provost (pages 8, 38): head of a Scottish town council, corresponding to a mayor.

reading heids (page 111): in the absence of tea leaves and Tarot cards, this was a peculiarly Scottish form of fortune telling in which the reader would feel "the lumps and bumps on a man's heid which were truly a mark of the life he would lead." This was very popular amongst the working people.

richt (pages 39, 44): right.

sartorial dress (page 79): relating to tailored clothes. The fishermen's dark blue 'uniforms' made the standard garb of the traditional caddies look shabby by comparison.

sicht (pages 44, 111): sight.

sillybodkins (pages 74, 75): The term *silly* can mean weak, shaky, or unsubstantial. A *bodkin* is a dagger, stiletto, or small, sharply-pointed instrument. Perhaps the screw nails were prone to fly out of the corks when given a good whack by an enthusiastic caddie!

skelp (page 64): a stroke or blow, especially with a flat object. In this case, a smack with the open hand.

spoon (page 66): a wooden golf club with a slightly hollowed head and backward-sloping face, corresponding to the number 3 wood (nineteenth to early twentieth century). Also known as scrapers, spoons came in short, middle and long sizes.

stumpie (page 80): a short, stocky or dumpy person.

stymie (page vi): difficulty in seeing things; making the best of bad luck. It was said that, "real life had its stymies," and perhaps through golf, we were encouraged to accept them philosophically.

tacket, tackety (page 82): A tacket is a small nail, latterly especially a hobnail, used to stud the soles of shoes, etc.

tae (pages 2, 4, 58, et al.): to.

twa (pages 23 [footnote], 90): two. Jock Hutchinson was given a "twa and six tip," meaning 2/6d or 12 new pence.

wan (pages 35, 91): one (numeral or pronoun).

wark (page 37): work.

wee nip (pages 1, 44, 62): a small quantity of liquor, usually whiskey. The word nip comes from *nipperkin*, a small wine and beer measure containing about half a pint or slightly less.

weel, wel (pages 39, 91): well.

whin (pages vii, 8, 54, et al.): the common furze or gorse; in plural, a clump or area of gorse. The whins have always been a primary hazard on the Old Course, and they provide one of its most outstanding visual features as well, because no matter what time of year, there is always some part of the foliage sporting golden flowers. An old Scottish saying has it that "when the whin's not in bloom, love's out of season."

widnae (page 58): would not.

wigging (pages 14, 15, 22, 115): severe censure from a person in authority; scolding or reprimand. This word might derive from the idea of being scolded by a wigged superior; e.g., a judge.

Wingy (pages 43, 125): To wingle means to hang loosely, dangle, flap or wag. By extension, men who had lost an arm in the war, and thus had a loose sleeve, were called 'Wingy.'

wisnae (page 91): was not.

workin' the tools (page 114): refers to a caddie who can club his man, given any shot.

yins (page 83): auld yins, young yins, wee yins refers to people in an affectionate or compassionate sense. Lang Willie would have been known as the 'Big Yin.'

Charlie Ferguson (left) and Jim Brown, 1997. Charlie joined the department as a seasonal assistant in 1996, and Jim has been the full-time Assistant Caddie Manager since 1995. When asked to rate his game, Charlie says, "Practice, practice and more practice!"

BIBLIOGRAPHY

Balfour, James. *Reminiscences of Golf on St. Andrews Links.* Edinburgh, 1887.

Burnett, Bobby, *The St. Andrews Opens.* London, 1990.

Chapman, Kenneth G. *The Rules of the Green: A History of the Rules of Golf.* Chicago, 1997.

Darwin, Bernard. *Golf.* London, 1954.

Elliot, Alan and John Allanman. *A History of Golf.* London, 1990.

The Evening Telegraph, Dundee, 1938.

Everard, H. S. C. *History of the Royal & Ancient Golf Club: St. Andrews, from 1754 to 1900.* Edinburgh, 1907.

Golf Illustrated, 1899-1940.

Herd, Sandy. *My Golfing Life.* London.

Hutchison, Horace G. *Fifty Years of Golf.* London, 1914.

Jarrett, Tom. *St. Andrews Golf Links: The First 600 Years.* Edinburgh, 1995.

Kirkaldy, Andrew. *My Fifty Years of Golf: Memories.* London, 1921.

Lang, Andrew. *Golfing Papers.*

MacKenzie, Alister. *The Spirit of St. Andrews.* Chelsea, MI, 1995.

Mackie, Keith. *Golf at St. Andrews.* London, 1995.

McPherson, J. Gordon. *Golf and Golfers.*

Robertson, J. K. *St. Andrews, Home of Golf.* St. Andrews, 1967.

Salmond, J. B. *The Story of the R&A.* London, 1956.

St. Andrews Citizen, 1890-1925.

Stirk, David. *Carry Your Bag, Sir?* London, 1996.

Taylor, Dawson. *St. Andrews, Cradle of Golf.*

Tullock, W. W. *Life of Tom Morris.* London, 1908.